What people are saying about

No One Playing

No One Playing is both a profound piece of work and a thoroughly enjoyable read. It's touching and truthful, skips along at a lovely pace, and is certainly not just for golfers too. It may just change the way you view the world and your 'self'.
Simon Mundie, broadcaster, event speaker and presenter of the BBC's 'Don't Tell Me the Score'.

I loved this short story. I read a hole each day diges⸍ the message or feel of the hole and then thinking abou⸍
Dr. Peter Evans, golfer, entrepreneur and doct⸍

It takes a certain type of golf book to ⸍ it to the end! Having played the g ⸍ng I tend to steer away from golf books. ⸍ ⸍his one. It's a great read and I think will be a ⸍ ⸍er for a lot of golfers at all levels. *No One Playing* gives ⸍t insight into the golfer's mind and what we go through out there.
    I know quite a few professional sports people are starting to see the benefits of mindfulness and *No One Playing* explains the process clearly and still keeps it relevant to golf.
Neil Rowlands, tournament professional golfer.

Wonderful! – this is lovely writing and story telling.
Dr Mark Davis, psychiatrist, golfer and long term meditator.

No One Playing

The essence of mindfulness and golf

No One Playing

The essence of mindfulness and golf

Martin Wells

MANTRA
BOOKS

Winchester, UK
Washington, USA

JOHN HUNT PUBLISHING

First published by Mantra Books, 2021
Mantra Books is an imprint of John Hunt Publishing Ltd., No. 3 East Street, Alresford
Hampshire SO24 9EE, UK
office@jhpbooks.com
www.johnhuntpublishing.com
www.mantra-books.net

For distributor details and how to order please visit the 'Ordering' section on our website.

ISBN: 978 1 78904 781 3
978 1 78904 782 0 (ebook)
Library of Congress Control Number: 2020947591

A CIP catalogue record for this book is available from the British Library.

Design: Stuart Davies

UK: Printed and bound by CPI Group (UK) Ltd, Croydon, CR0 4YY
Printed in North America by CPI GPS partners

We operate a distinctive and ethical publishing philosophy in
all areas of our business, from our global network of authors to
production and worldwide distribution.

Contents

Also by the author

Sitting in the Stillness
Mantra Books, John Hunt Publishing – Feb 2020

To Jack, my Dad, although he passed away almost thirty years ago his inspiration and love for the game has always stayed with me.

Acknowledgements

My heartfelt thanks to Sue, my wife, for all the love and encouragement and for sharing her wonderful writer's wisdom in the crafting and editing of this book.

Vielen Dank to my 97-year-old mum, Sabine, for her optimistic attitude to life, for her amazing resilience through thick and thin and her love of golf.

Thanks to my brother Tony for sharing the wonder of this great game and for all his generosity.

Also to Vaughn Malcolm (ex Oxford) and Charlie Nutbrown (ex Cambridge) for so generously giving up their time, doing such a brilliant job editing and for their encouraging feedback.

To my golfing, meditating Kiwi 'twin' Mark Davis for all the support and encouraging comments.

Merci Beaucoup to Jean-Marc Mantel for pointing me so clearly to the non-dual presence inspiring the main theme of the book.

Thanks to golf buddy Phil Norman for regularly getting up at the crack of dawn to play, for all the conversations about technique, mindfulness and the inner game.

To Peter Evans for the great feedback and the idea of a map at the beginning of each chapter.

Also to John Hunt Publishing for taking on this and my previous book *Sitting in the Stillness* and especially to Gavin Davies for his energy and enthusiasm in marketing both of them.

Prologue

This book is a story about a strange encounter on the golf course with someone who, on the face of it, knows nothing about golf but who ends up teaching me about the inner game and questioning my approach to golf and to life itself. So it is not just about golf, or sport. It's not about improvement or progress or how to do something. If anything, it points to a way of living effortlessly that is free and harmonious, that is, to the essence of mindfulness.

There's a saying 'Golf is a great teacher!' My companion for the day quickly understands this and uses the game as a metaphor for all sorts of lessons. He highlights the capacity for golf to teach the golfer not just about playing the game but about the performance of any task and about life in general. He offers deep insights into the workings of the mind and the power of the mind to inhibit and distort – about ego and humility – about the inter-connectedness of the natural world – about searching for answers and about the freedom that can be found by giving up the search, even about the fundamental question 'If we're not our thoughts who or what are we?'

His deep questioning goes to the heart of the game. For example, Why play? What really matters? What do you love about it?

These are questions that are not only about golf but about life – questions that radically shake up our comfortable status quo and potentially shatter our illusions. On this theme my mentor for the day also uses the example of the Covid-19 pandemic and how our usual patterns have been disrupted in order to highlight what is real and sustainable and what is not. He suggests that globally we have been invited to face these questions, as it were, in a lengthy and enforced mindfulness retreat.

In this way he suggests I come to see playing golf as meditation and all of life's activities as a mindfulness practice.

1

Introduction

Changing

Only one thing is certain–impermanence.
Buddha

Locker rooms often seem to be darker than they need to be. Almost holy. Lockers the colour of pews, musty smells, hushed tones, evoking a belief that one day the kingdom will be entered. Dank rooms adorned with the mundane: the odd wet sock, the abandoned broken umbrella, the pair of shoes that spiders have lived in since the days of Peter Alliss and Dai Rees.

This changing room floor was covered in tiny indentations caused by millions of spiked shoes over the last hundred years – testimonies to the countless hopes and dreams and golfing stories that had been told and experienced in these rooms. All that was left were the little marks, memories embedded in the atmosphere of the changing room.

'Changing' room seemed appropriate. These rooms and others had witnessed the mild-mannered change into monsters with golf clubs in their hands, brain surgeons into nervous wrecks, the competent into the incompetent, the clumsy into the most delicate, pussycats into tigers.

There was a note on my locker room door: ***Sorry can't make it, got flu, Tony.***

With many other sports I would have been left with little choice. No one to hit the ball back. No challenge to my strength, courage, cunning or stamina. With golf there is always the option of playing by yourself, of pitting your wits and skills against the course and the elements.

My decision was instant, although I went through some other possibilities: go to work and finish that report, do the week's supermarket shop. Who was I kidding?

I had been looking forward to playing for days and had already played much of the round in my imagination. I also had a strong but intangible sense that something was drawing me out there.

Every golfer knows that the course in itself provides a challenge and one that can be part of our personal relationship to it. Each course has a unique personality, and for a man his golf course is probably female! Will she still love me? What do I have to do to please her? How did I displease her? Why does she turn against me when things are going well? What mood is she in today?

As golfers we know that we are rarely in control. As soon as we think we are that is the time to be wary of the game's ability to remind us of our capacity for humiliation and our vulnerability. No professional golfer says 'I'm playing really well and will win this week'. This is partly because the pro golfer is a member of a superstitious breed but partly because they know that form can leave you overnight like an overly-sensitive lover. Much better to replay the worn-out clichés 'I'll just take each shot as it comes' or 'I hope the golfing gods are with me'. I guess the game, in this way, can teach respect for the environment and a healthy version of humility.

Without an opponent, the weather on the links can turn out to be the true challenger. A seaside course can play differently almost every time you go out. Today the wind was off the sea, light but getting up, enough to make a difference to the club selection. Enough to invite the faster swing, the big swipe at the ball, or the attempt to steer it. All fatal to the result.

Enough, also, to set off the excitement in my stomach, making the decision a foregone conclusion. Maybe today I would learn the secret, everything falling into place. The swing adjustment I made last time seemed to work. I'll try that. The sweet high of addiction. Do I forget that the lows are wrapped up in the same parcel? Or am I addicted to those as well?

The wind rattled one of the windows that faced the sea. It felt like a warning from the elements.

'You may think you can plan your round from the cosy warmth of the locker room. Come out here and let me blow you off balance! Let me make your eyes water as you fix your gaze on the ball. Let me nudge that beautifully flighted nine iron into the bunker next to the pin.'

I had found the ball that I wanted to use and had placed it on the bench next to me, balanced on one of its dimples. Golf balls had originally been smooth and it was an accidental discovery that a ball with little indentations travelled more truly to its target. Before that, the old gutta percha ball had been invented by a Scottish golfing Reverend who had ordered a statue of Vishnu, the Hindu god, from India. It came wrapped in the rubbery gutta percha substance to protect it, and the good Reverend found that he could mould it into a golf ball to supersede the feathery. Maybe God intervened and maybe Vishnu too!

Before this 'divine' intervention the golf ball was made of feathers (about a top hat full) stuffed tightly into a small leather pouch and sewn up. They took a while to make and had to be abandoned when they became sodden with water.

As I looked at my ball, I remembered fragments of a dream from the night before. In it I had been intently marking my card on the eighteenth green. I was muttering to myself about missed opportunities and mistakes. I looked up so that the expletive leaving my lips could be projected into the air. As I did, I noticed with horror that the player behind me had miscued his shot to the green. His ball was flying directly towards my head at high speed but before striking me slowed down to almost no speed at all. Just before it struck me smack between my eyes, I could clearly make out a green and white and blue pattern on the ball. In the split second before impact I recognised it as the earth.

The ball knocked me unconscious and I was sent spinning

amongst the stars. I had become the earth and was floating, turning and orbiting in a vast universe. It was beautiful and awesome. In the dream I came to on the course and had fully recovered except that the ball was still lodged in the middle of my forehead. Rather than this being a problem, it appeared to improve my vision in a bizarre way. I could no longer see anything as separate from anything else. Everything was connected.

I woke up at this point and although I had lost the sense of connection, I could still feel, like a finger pressing there, the place where I had been struck between the eyebrows. (What was that about?)

I picked up the ball on my way out of the changing room and headed for the course. The clicking of the steel spikes on the concrete floor helped bring me out of my daydream.

Holding the ball in my hand I was more aware than ever before of the firm roundness of the beautifully engineered modern golf ball.

Designed to fly.

Chapter 1

The First

The length of a golf course is five and a half inches – the space between your ears.
Bobby Jones

The crunch of gravel underneath my feet seemed much louder than usual and the early morning mist against the skin on my face almost hurt. Dew hung on bended grass and no other footprints spoilt the challenge I was relishing. I imagined the excitement of mountaineers treading virgin snow.

Only as I approached the first tee did I notice the figure. The incongruity of the man's appearance should have been remarkable to me but, in a way, I was not at all surprised to see him there. His jet black hair glistened in the watery sunlight and his cotton collarless shirt was striking in its whiteness and its uniqueness as attire for the golf course. Sandals would not have been my first choice as footwear either, and his toes already glistened with the moisture from the grass he had walked through.

He was about 5ft 4in and stocky. His skin was a beautiful rich brown, a mixture of brown and gold.

His face was hard to place geographically. Malaysia, Tibet, India?

The smile was broad and the crow's feet well worn. He could have been anywhere between 30 and 60.

'Morning.'

'Good morning to you, Sir,' he replied, with the faintest of bows.

'You playing?'

'No, no, no,' the man chuckled about this question, which he clearly thought absurd and went on:

'Please no, I am visiting my brother here in your country and he told me about your game of golf and I became interested and thought to come and see for myself before I return home.'

'Would you like to walk round with me?' I heard myself saying. I didn't think through this offer at all but as I looked into his rich brown eyes, it felt like an imperative, as though I was hypnotised.

'I would like that very much, thank you.'

In these few words was struck this strange pairing which was to turn my approach to the game I love upside down and inside out. I was going to see a familiar object completely as new, just as a tiny child lives in pure experience before words come along to create a world of separate things.

Only as I stood over the first shot did I consider the implications of playing with someone who knew nothing of the game. Would I have to explain everything? Would I be able to concentrate? What made me invite him?

* * *

The first hole starts inland and then bears sharp left following the line of the seashore. In golfing language: a dog leg. Unless the player is aiming for safety the first shot of the round needs to go over the edge of the beach. The more he or she aims to shorten the hole the more beach there is to carry. The dunes stretch away into the distance and the pungent smell of the sea is often the first thing you notice as you climb on to the exposed tee.

Standing up on the little flat square of crisply mown turf, I surveyed the expanse of sea before me. This aspect was never the same. The angle of the sun, the thickness of the mist, the swell of the sea and the movement of the tide always contrived to make me look each time as though for the first time. Today the island that lay some ten miles away sat brooding under the mist, dark and distant. On clear days I felt it so close that I could have reached out and touched the steep hillsides or at least sailed a seven-iron shot across the straits.

The green is over 400 yards away and hidden behind a mound, so that only the flag is visible. The undulating green is a challenge in itself and par is not assured by being on the surface in two.

The tee itself was in lovely condition, very firm and a little sandy under foot and cut really short. I chose a wooden tee peg which took some pressure to put in the ground; the ball sitting on it looked very inviting. I was doing these things without thought and started to wonder again what my guest would need to know and how much I would need to explain.

As I swung the club my new companion stood very still from some intuitive sense of the right thing to do; the ball went straight but not very far. I had made a reasonable swing but not got the timing right. We saw it skim low over the beach, land and bounce two to three times on to the fairway about 190 yards away.

I set off in the direction of the ball and he followed. As we negotiated the steep slope down from the tee to my clubs and the fairway, I noticed the sandals that the man was wearing. I was thinking that he would really struggle to keep his balance on the dewy slopes of grass when I saw how easily he seemed to be moving, as though he weighed ten times more than me or had some special relationship to the ground. It struck me as odd, but I thought no more of it at this stage.

'Beautiful morning!' he beamed at me.

'Yes, my favourite time to be out on the links.'

'The links?'

'Yes, it is the original word for the seaside golf course, where the soil is sandy and dry and few trees grow. Inland courses are on park or heathland.' I had no idea of how much he wanted to know so carried on.

'A links is the oldest style of golf course, first developed in Scotland. The word "links" comes via the Scots language from the Old English word hlinc: "rising ground, ridge".'

'I see, thank you,' he said, looking genuinely interested.

'Does the word link not also mean connection?'

'Yes, it does,' I said with authority as though I'd already made that 'link' myself.

'I'm going to play a whole round,' I said.

'Excuse me but why is this called a round?'

His politeness did nothing for the first sense of mild irritation I felt welling up in me. Would there be a thousand questions like this? Would I still be able to concentrate on my game? Why did he want to know?

Part of my irritation was that I'd never really asked myself the question. The feeling reminded me of the times when my daughter had asked all those questions in the 'why are leaves green, Daddy?' category. My mundane reply reflected the lack of thought that I'd previously applied to this innocent question.

'Well, as you play the course you come back round to where you started from.'

He laughed in a way that I was to become very familiar with over the morning. It was a sort of deep chuckle starting in the belly and then shaking his whole body.

'Then, my friend, your game is like life: in my culture the circle or round symbolises the wheel of life. We may go round many times making the same mistakes, learning new lessons, meeting ourselves again and again, searching for answers and meanings.'

My first thought was that it was too early in the morning for such profundity. This type of conversation was not what I'd had in mind for today's game – more a chance to practise a few revisions to my swing.

But then I started to think about other 'rounds' in golf:

swinging round your body, a round ball into a round hole. He'd set in motion a whole string of thoughts.

I also started to think about my life off the course and those things that had come round and round again until I finally faced them. I found it strange to be thinking about golf as a part of my life and of me, as opposed to something that I 'did'. I usually did not consider my other life on the links but was used to immersing myself in the game as a distraction from the everyday.

'What is the purpose of this game?'

I initially thought this an easier question, until I found more and more layers to it, rather like saying a familiar word repeatedly until it sounds entirely strange and new to the ear.

To make a good score... to win... for the fresh air... for the walking... for the company... as character building... addiction... better than shopping... for the joy of sending the ball to the target...

'There are many purposes,' I said, playing for time.

My companion appeared happy with this answer. I suspected that something straightforward would have been met with a knowing and sceptical smile.

We had arrived at my ball, which was lying on a slight downslope on the dry brown grass. I could see the top of the pin about 175 yards away in the distance. The flag fluttered frenetically. The wind was off the sea. The chill in the morning air encouraged me to get swinging and my practice swings were vigorous. My eyes watered as the bite in the breeze caught my face. The second shot is always blind apart from the flag. I could not see all the humps and hollows en route or the bunker that guarded the undulating green.

I thought I could probably reach with a five iron but, considering that I had not warmed up, chose a four.

In anticipation of the question that never came I started to think about how I would describe the fourteen golfing implements known as clubs. How would I explain that the same word is also used for the place and course where people are members. I once heard that a young man was given a golf club for his twenty-first birthday present and not being that impressed until I realised that they meant an entire Cornish golf course.

For some reason the 'sticks' of steel or graphite and rubber in my golf bag were also called clubs. It made me think of our cave-dwelling ancestors. The way different players swung these implements also suggested different names: for example, weapons, scythes, magic wands.

Golf clubs have been developed for hundreds of years; we know that James VI of Scotland instructed his bow maker to make him some golf clubs in 1603. Legend has it that a shepherd was the first to use his crook as a club as he attempted to knock a stone down a rabbit hole. Since that time bits of wood and metal have been fixed onto other bits of wood or metal to allow the golfer to hit the ball different distances and heights: to roll the ball; to hit it long distances; to get it out of sand and so on.

Should I tell this bloke all this stuff? No, it's probably just for the golfing nerds amongst us. More pieces of history surfaced.

The first golfers had between six and nine clubs in their bags but by the 1930s some were carrying up to thirty. A rule was understandably introduced limiting us all to fourteen. Even this number allowed for a range of implements that meant that a golfer could make almost the same swing with two different clubs but that one would propel the ball low and fast over 250 yards and the other make the ball rise slowly and steeply landing softly from a great height about 80 yards away. The other clubs made the ball go the yardages in between and with such accuracy that, these days, that a professional's caddie will know the distance to the hole to the nearest yard.

These thoughts were still percolating as I swung the club back okay but when I arrived at the top of the swing another thought occurred to me. 'This is too much club so don't hit it too hard.' Thinking in this way immediately impacted on my body, so that I got over tense, came down more with hands and arms holding back on the movement of legs and hips. The end result was a flat, sharply bending flight to the left, a hook, which only stayed in bounds thanks to the heavy dew in the rough that had an effect like air brakes on my errant ball – the ball which was otherwise heading for the beach as though there was only one deckchair left empty on a sunny bank holiday.

'I knew I was going to do that,' I said out loud with some venom. I had completely forgotten that I had a non-playing guest and I was even more embarrassed when this aroused his interest.

'Was this not an outcome you were wanting?' he asked.

'No, it wasn't the outcome I was wanting,' I replied, hoping that he did not hear the irony in my voice.

'And yet you knew you were going to do it?' he said very pleasantly, going, in his first ten minutes on the course, to the heart of a golfer's dilemma. This could really get under my skin!

There was a pause.

Of course, if I knew I was going to do it, why did I? If only we knew the answer to that one.

On every course in every round, golfers will no doubt be occasionally envisaging the disaster before or during the swing, then producing the result in the next few seconds of body movement. This is commonly followed by the phrase 'I knew I was going to do that' or variations on that theme like: 'I always do that here; I can never play that shot.'

His comment also made me think that this mindset applies not only to the individual shots but sometimes to the whole round, as in 'It is not my day' (predicted on the second green) or 'If I don't start well there is no chance'.

I started to wonder about the great golfers and how they learnt how to manage the negative thoughts. Players like Seve

Ballesteros and now Tiger Woods have made the impossible possible with the power of mind linked to technique.

I almost stepped on my ball in the thick rough but would probably not have found it had I not been so close. It was buried deep.

'Here it is!' I called out.

'The things we search for are often right where we are.' He said, looking pleased with his little aphorism.

I was only three yards from the small dunes that marked the beginning of the beach. The sea spray buffeted my face and the smell of seaweed was in my nostrils. Oystercatchers skipped along the sand barely touching it as though crossing red-hot coals. The last tide's debris lay in a semicircle along the beach, bits of driftwood and plastic bottles.

A message in one of the bottles about how to play this next shot would have been welcome. The face on my sand wedge disappeared as I addressed the ball. The grass was very wet and would slow the club head. I looked up at the shot I had to play. I only had sixty yards to the pin but a small pot bunker lay in front of the green directly in my line. The sensible 'percentage' shot would have been to aim wide of the bunker for the apron of the green but I was more interested in the glory shot (the fool's option).

I used the sort of force that off the fairway would have propelled the ball over 100 yards, but which now caused the ball to hop feebly out of the deep grass towards the green, landing five yards short of the bunker then trickling into it. Suddenly the percentage shot seemed much more attractive. My new companion was standing quite close to the bunker and watched the ball on its sad little journey. The look on his face was one of curiosity. 'It has arrived in this little beach,' he remarked.

'Yes, thank you, it has,' was my terse reply.

The bunker allowed room for only one person to stand in and was deep with a steep face. The sand was smooth and well raked. Having rolled slowly in, my ball lay in a good place at the back of the sand. Bunker shots generally hold no fear for me and I picked a spot two inches behind the ball and made a smooth wristy swing. The ball popped up high, landed with a little thud and released down to three feet from the hole.

Occasionally this game feels easy, I thought. I quickly reminded myself that there were other shots that did scare me (for example, chipping over the bunker). As my thoughts returned to an earlier theme, I wondered what difference it would make if I were to approach these shots with the same ease and confidence.

The normally quick putt was made much easier by the heavy dew and I was able to make a firm stroke and to hear the result as the ball rattled into the hole.

'This is the purpose?' my 'gallery' enquired.

'Yes, this is the purpose,' I said, abruptly.

But his quaint English meant I found myself relating to the game a little differently. It also raised the possibility of the absurd nature of the sport! I could hear my wife's pleading refrain:

'Why do you do it?' I knew the answer was something to do with love but at this point that was the best I could come up with. For some reason I had a sense I would know more by the end of this morning's experience.

Chapter 2

The Second

The problem was the thought: 'What if this goes wrong?'
Jonny Wilkinson in conversation with Simon Mundie on the
BBC's podcast 'Don't Tell Me the Score'

From the first green the course begins to set off inland. There
is a little climb to the second, enough to increase the heart rate
and expand the lungs. The tee is exposed to any wind and one's
arrival is usually greeted with a blast and the accompanying
watery eyes.

This was true for me today and I was particularly in touch
with a surge of exhilaration that formed a part of my love for
the game and its challenges: the elements, the course as it rolls
over natural terrain, as well as hazards that against which I
would pit my skill, physical capacities and wit.

The second fairway is generous in width but rolls like a
crumpled blanket in its undulating travel towards the green.
Golfers disappear and reappear in its folds. They can either
be heard playing invisible shots from in between the hillocks
or spotted attempting to replicate their usual golf swing with
one foot planted eighteen inches higher than the other. It is one
of those holes where, apart from the occasional invisible shot,
you can see the whole thing from the tee, the experiences of the
players in front of me unfolding like a soap opera, often tragic
sometimes sublime. A relative of mine is intensely irritated by
the use of the word 'tragic' in relation to sport... 'Tragic,' he
says is for human suffering not for taking seven shots when
six would win you the Open. Jean van der Velde said as much
himself having done just that in 1999.

* * *

The green about 370 yards away, is convex and tipped up to face you. It is inviting but surprisingly difficult to get your ball on and then manage to stay on, especially in summer and when it is dry. Bunkers protect either side. Today the wind was helping. Into the wind this hole could demand two full wood shots for the best of players. I reasoned that the best play today was an easy three wood, get it into the air and let the breeze do the rest. A reasonable strike should leave me something like a seven or eight iron into the green. I had selected my club and began to wonder where my companion was. As he was new to the game, I didn't want him endangering himself or distracting me. Or was I more concerned about him distracting me than him endangering himself?

I saw that he'd sauntered off and was standing on a hillock about forty yards away. He looked away from the hole and faced into the wind. His jet-black hair flowed behind him like a horse's mane and he was staring intensely as though he could see something in the wind itself. He was transfixed, like a baby, totally absorbed. I remembered watching my daughter as a baby gazing without interruption at a leaf fluttering in the breeze for a full twenty minutes at that stage of still really seeing before the clutter of language and categorisation interrupts the experience.

I decided to play, but half wondered whether to let him know or not. A person's focus on the links is usually on the game, so his behaviour was a little disconcerting.

I teed the ball up low and addressed it, standing a little wider than usual to be well anchored in the breeze. I made a reasonable swing back, but on the way down, tried to hit the ball in the air rather than allowing the club head to do the work. The result was the opposite of what I'd intended. I came up a little quickly and caught the top half of the ball, setting it off really low. It avoided all radar systems but ran into a problem at the first fairway hillock, crashing into the side of it full pelt. All momentum was lost and instead of carrying another seventy yards or so it popped upwards on the hillside and came to rest four to five yards beyond its pitch mark.

I picked up my bag and walked over to my acquaintance. He took a couple of skipping steps down from his hillock. As if from his daydream state, he said:

'I'm sorry but I am thinking I still do not understand the purpose of this game,'

Okay well... to finish the game with a good score or having beaten your opponent.'

'So, the purpose is the ending?'

'Yes, I suppose so!' A skylark flapped vigorously nearby; a lot of effort expended in going nowhere.

'Strange,' he said, 'Does that mean your destination in life is death?'

I was dumbstruck. I had only met him 10 minutes ago and he was diving straight into the meaning of my life and assuming that golf had something to do with it.

'It's only a game,' I said with some force and immediately felt as though I was twelve years old again trying to defend myself against my Chemistry teacher's charge of having just set light to Bintliffe's briefcase.

He backed off, 'I'm sorry, you are right.'

However, I got the distinct impression that he had retreated out of politeness. But did he mean it?

As I was thinking this, I noticed the sturdiness of his frame. He had the walk of a much heavier man. I remembered hearing of certain Tai Chi masters who challenged five strong men to push them over. The master remained standing. Perhaps he was a man who would only give way on his terms.

I stomped down the fairway with a hollow-legged victory, cursing myself that I was so curious to know what he meant. I had my next shot to play, an ample distraction from this uncomfortable exchange.

Part of this distraction was to figure out how to stand given that the ball was resting on a one in three incline some 170 yards from the putting surface. 'It's only a game,' I repeated silently to myself as I found the most comfortable stance I could muster. Keen to prove my point, my swing was aimless and carefree but in a loose, slack way. The club face and ball barely made contact and the result was a dullish clacking thud. It sent the ball off at about 10 mph, cutting sharply before slithering shamefully into deep grass 120 yards away. I went from 'It's only a game' to 'It's a matter of life and death' in a millisecond and threw the club in the same direction as the ball... and nearly as far. I recalled the late Bill Shankly once saying 'football is not a matter of life and death; it is more serious than that.'

The instant the club left my hand and swished off into the sky my last words about it only being a game rang in my ears. I couldn't look at him and only hoped that he saw this as one of the game's quirkier procedures.

I also couldn't not look at him and sneaked a quick peek. He looked into my eyes and smiled. There was no hint of ridicule, but I thought I glimpsed something like acceptance. For a brief instant I felt sort of washed by that look. There seemed nothing to say. I felt I would know more as this round progressed.

The feeling lasted for a few moments and I almost floated into the rough with my sand iron in hand and no thoughts in my head. The swing I made was easy and perfectly timed. My ball sailed out of the rough, took no notice of the green and landed on a path a full 60 yards beyond it. The end result was dreadful, but this didn't seem to matter one bit. The smooth swing and the crisp strike had been sublime.

There was no question but that I had to play my ball off the path, which was an integral part of the course. No free drop would be available in the rules. It was one of those shots that you often feel better about later in the round, when in a bit of a rhythm, as it requires a very accurate strike. Nearer the end of the round you can start feeling a little sharper about these ones.

However, I got lucky and got the club flange to the bottom of the ball, squeezing it against the little gravel stones of the path at impact. The effect of these stones was like the action of the pimples on a table tennis bat, imparting extra spin. The flight of the ball was low and it landed level with the pin about four foot right. At this stage the shot looked much too long but because of the extra spin the ball hopped another six feet and then stopped on the spot as if using air brakes. I was left with a putt back up the hill of about seven feet. Many pros have perfected this sort of chip without the aid of gravel. I thought to myself that I'm going to continue to need the gravel.

A putt for a five, I reasoned, would be an escape after some indifferent shots. This thought, however, had me counting the shot before I had played it and in so doing imagining a six if I missed. I read the putt correctly and stroked it firmly at the left lip of the hole. However, my pre-putt thoughts had induced a little extra urgency and too much pace in my putting stroke. The ball raced through the borrow and across the side of the hole. I now had two feet coming back. Downhill, fast with a slight borrow. Do I pick up? Is it a gimme? After all, I'm on my own. Mr Asktoomuch would be bound to want to know why I had not put the little white fellow below ground.

I decided to putt it, but had not committed to doing this properly and to going through my usual routine. The effect was a stance not properly aligned and a rather nudgy little putting stroke, which sent the ball on a hesitating descent, like a guilty boy on the way to the headmaster's office. Missed. I tapped in for a seven. More red mist flashed in front of my eyes and I attempted to half volley the ball cricket fashion off the green. Only on the second attempt did I make contact, with a satisfying 'Ping', sending the ball towards the next tee.

My satisfaction was short-lived as, first the ball landed short of the tee in some very long grass and second, because my witness for the day would no doubt want to understand the finer points of my tantrum.

I headed off, hoping that if I made no eye contact, he might leave me alone to stew in my own juice. Undaunted, he came up to me overflowing with curiosity. It was almost as though I was inviting this attention at the times that were most challenging for me to deal with.

'You can throw and hit?' he asked.

'No.'

'But?'

'I was angry. I was expressing... it was a tantrum.'

'Ah.' He seemed to understand. 'We have tantra,' he said. 'It is to do with self-expression, action. What is in should come out. This is the same?'

'No. I don't know. I doubt it,' I muttered.

'Yes, I think maybe so,' he insisted.

This could become really irritating. My fuse was already short.

'Look, why do you need to talk about everything. Sometimes things just happen!' I snapped.

'No, my friend, nothing **just** happens. This a big difference between Eastern and Western man. Western man thinks his life is a random set of happenings. He walks along a beach and something washes up next to him and he says, "What a coincidence!" Eastern man asks, "Why has this particular object washed up at this time next to me?"' He hesitated.

'Do you think our meeting this morning is coincidence?'

'Yes, of course! Why, did you plan it?'

'With respect, you are missing the point. Neither of us planned it but perhaps there is some meaning in our meeting, perhaps other forces are at work in us, arranging and orchestrating behind the scenes.'

'I can't believe that,' I said, walling out any possibility of what he described.

'I'm not asking you to believe it,' he replied with the same firmness in his voice as earlier.

'Experience it! Ask yourself the meaning of the meetings you've had, of the events that have occurred in your life.'

'Okay, my wife has just had a major operation and been on crutches for eight months... what is the meaning of that?' I brought out my trump card. He was unfazed.

'I don't know,' he said quite openly. 'But let us just assume for a moment that you had both in some way organised this for your own good. What came out of it?'

'Pain, hard work, discomfort, fear, loss of income and lots more!' I could not see where this was leading but continued to look for my ball in the long grass next to the tee. I was adding a bit of vigour to the swishing of the club as I hunted for the little ******.

'Yes, yes, I'm sure and I'm sorry for this, but what came out of it for you and she. What gifts?' he persisted. The words dog and bone came to mind.

I finally stopped to really consider his question at the level intended. I found my ball at the same moment.

'Well. We got a lot closer over that time. There was more tenderness between us. My wife learned to depend on me as never before. I learned to look after myself at the same time as looking after her.' The thoughts spilled out of me like coins from a fruit machine.

He smiled a wide smile but not with a look of triumph so much as fundamental certainty.

'Have you not noticed the potential for change that has come from our worldwide pandemic?'

'Yes, I have and all the suffering.'

'Very true! There has been great suffering, as you describe with you and your wife although on a much smaller scale. The suffering also had the function of waking us up from many illusions – from the illusion of separateness reminding us that we are all connected and that there are consequences to our actions, meaning that we are not free to do what we want – waking us from the myth that we are not really harming the planet. Notice how the natural world loved humans being prevented from polluting the earth. In my country you could swim in the Ganges for the first time in several lifetimes.' Tears were rolling down his cheeks at this point but they did not interrupt him only seeming to fuel the passion in his words. 'People reached out to each other regardless of age and the colour of their skin and many risked their own lives to save others.'

His words did not seem to invite a reply. It was as though he had rung a big bell; the deep sound resonated right through me and slowly faded in the silence that followed.

Chapter 3

The Third

The tasting of the pure atmosphere and the working of limb and muscle are splendid things, enough to justify any day and any game, but no golfer is heard to put them in the forefront of the advantages he has derived from his day's participation in the game unless the golf he has played has been miserably disappointing.
Harry Vardon 1905

Having found my ball by the tee I followed the steep, narrow path to the level of the tee box. Only on reaching this spot did I get the view of the third hole, a mere 130 yards from tee to green but with a deep little valley of long grass in between. The only areas of short grass in the vicinity are the tee and the green. In between and all around is tall grass and some gorse bushes with their bright yellow sickly-scented flowers.

Miss the green right or short and you could be in all sorts of trouble. The wind was off the sea and blowing left to right but standing on the tee I was a little protected from the breeze by the huge dunes. I figured that a high-flying ball would be less protected and therefore more affected in its flight. Having settled on a nine iron, I aimed slightly left of the green, aware that anything less than a really good strike would be severely punished. As the ball left the club face, I felt quite pleased. I had made a good contact and the ball headed off towards the left side of the green. However, as soon as it got above the height of the dunes the wind kicked in and drifted the ball to the right. It still managed to land on the putting surface but on the edge of the green. After bouncing quite high once, it rolled around the rim of the green side bunker and started to trickle down the steep slope at the right of the green. Gathering momentum now it headed down into the valley and finished in deep grass some 30 feet below the green.

'****! What bad luck!' I exclaimed.

I looked at my new 'friend' with some hope for sympathy and support. Even an opponent might have empathised with this experience and uttered some words of comfort. Instead out came another story:

'Many years ago, I had a friend whose only horse ran away. That evening his neighbours came to commiserate with him saying that this was such bad luck. He replied, "Maybe." The next day the horse returned with six wild horses. The neighbours came to celebrate saying what good luck. The farmer said, "Maybe." The next day, the farmer's son rode one of the horses, was thrown and broke his leg. Once again, the neighbours offered support, saying, "What bad luck!" and once again he said, "Maybe." The next day army officials came to the village conscripting young men to the army. His son was not taken because of his injury...'

He smiled as he told the story and I noticed a different sort of comfort from being supported in my misery although couldn't really describe it. I also fully expected to find a £20 note next to my ball.

If there had been such a note it would have been pretty difficult to find given the length of the grass that my ball had come to rest in. The grass just around the ball was not too bad making it look deceptively easy to make contact. Also, around it, however, was that long wispy grass that appears innocuous but try and get a golf club through it and it will wrap itself around the club and almost wrench it from your grip.

This is exactly what happened. The ball flew off really low and about 30 degrees off line. Right on cue came my piece of luck. The ball was caught by the rim of the bunker, ran around the edge like on a wall of death at a funfair and span out back on line. Still travelling too fast, it sped past the hole like a busy commuter on his way to work. The steep bank at the back of the green killed its momentum, stopped it and sent it rolling slowly, grudgingly back onto the green about 20 feet from the hole.

The words 'How lucky' seemed to ring out between us but neither wanted to invite the next turn of fate. The smile on his face seemed broader and I thought I detected a slight nod of the head.

I was faced with a straightish putt but down a steep slope. Immediately I remembered the last green and the problems I had got into. A whole conversation began in my head along the lines of 'Don't do this' and 'Don't do that' so that by the time it came to making a putting stroke, the movement was mostly made up of don'ts. I barely set the ball rolling and it crept down the hill and stopped two feet short of the cup. The events of my last putting experience were all too vivid at that moment and I started to have some more of those 'Don't do that again' thoughts. This was undoubtedly the worst preparation for this tricky little putt and the jerky movement that passed for a putting stroke had no chance of sending the ball to its proper destination. It didn't even go near the hole but miserably dribbled by.

'You ****ing idiot!' I muttered to myself, the inner critic in his element.

My personal pantomime villain piping up with another moral admonishment. At least they didn't come with the sort of violence that featured in the first morality stories that were read to me aged four. (Vivid images included!) They came from a book called Struwwelpeter originally written in 1845. The most terrifying story was about the boy (about my age) who was warned about sucking his thumb when his parents were not around. He did and out from behind the curtains came a demonic figure with a pair of scissors that were three times bigger than the boy. The next illustration shows the boy without his thumbs and blood spurting like a fountain from the stumps. There was still a version of this sort of demon that lurked in the shadows of my mind and jumped out on the golf course from time to time.

Thankfully, my new companion did not seem prone to this style of story.

I wasn't sure whether he'd heard my mutterings but what he then said, on reflection, seemed relevant.

'I'm sorry if I offended you a few minutes ago,' he said. 'I hope you will forgive me?'

'Yes, of course,' I said, thinking how formal and polite he seemed.

'And yourself too?'

I felt exposed and embarrassed. I didn't want to be having this sort of conversation on the golf course or anywhere else for that matter, or want to be faced with another uncomfortable truth. I do not easily forgive myself either on or off the course and could be harshly self-critical. It wasn't as if the self-criticism was constructive. I usually just felt ashamed, defensive and as a result switched off from any lessons to be learnt.

He suddenly said, 'There were once two ex-prisoners of war talking. One asked the other, "Have you forgiven your captors?"

'"No," the other replied.

'"Then they still have you in prison!"'

This story got me thinking about how much freer I'd feel over the shot I was about to play if I'd forgiven myself for the previous one. Sometimes this would not have even been the last shot I was thinking about. I might have even been stewing over a fluffed chip from three holes ago. It occurred to me that if I were my own gaoler then it followed that I could free myself!

A couple of days earlier a friend had told me that some tennis players wave their hands in front of their faces like a windscreen wiper after a poor shot to clear away the image from the brain. Sometimes I think I need bleach and a scrubbing brush!

Chapter 4

The Fourth

Many acts are most successfully carried out when they are not the object of particularly concentrated attention... mistakes may occur just on those occasions when one is most eager to be accurate.
Sigmund Freud, *A General Introduction to Psychoanalysis*

I was still chuntering to myself about the last putt as I reached the next tee. At least I thought it was to myself as he seemed too far away to hear me.

'Keep your head down!'

'You are telling yourself to do something?'

'Yes.'

'Is it a new instruction?'

'No! I have told myself this thousands of times.'

'I see.'

The pause after his response was filled with possibility. The version I had going on in the gap was, 'Well, you must be pretty damn stupid if you give yourself a simple instruction over and over again which you can't remember to act on!'

'You are telling your body to do something?' he asked.

'Yes!' The more he asked and the more I thought about it, the dafter this all seemed. Surely, I am in charge of my body enough to give it a simple instruction. Sometimes it might be the only swing thought in my mind and yet my head would still come up.

'Perhaps the mind is involved?'

'With respect, you have never played this game. So how could you possibly understand the mechanics of how to play!'

'You are right.' And then as if he could not help himself: 'But it sounds like it might be more than mechanics?'

He was irritatingly persistent but without the sort of energy where he needed to be right, more as though he was there to teach me something.

That somehow made it worse and harder to hold my position which, of course, was right!

'Well of course it's not just that, but if you get the mechanics and the technique right then the rest will follow,' I said, authoritatively.

'If that were true then why are you telling your body to do something thousands of times with not much success?' he said. 'I presume that you have learnt a successful technique that has worked many times.'

'Yes, of course!'

'Then maybe it is your mind that does not trust the technique,' he said and paused.

'So then,' he continued, 'the thought influences the body. You are afraid of failure so the mind no longer trusts the body. If it has worked well before why do you not trust it to work well again?'

He looked at me directly.

'When there is fear,' he explained, 'your mind will influence your body and your head comes up to see the result. Which might explain why no matter how many times you tell your body to do something, if the mind is agitated then problems occur.'

'Okay, but how come it works sometimes and not others?'

'Perhaps because having a consistent thought provides a sort of security and confidence.'

'A sort of security?'

'Yes, but it is actually an illusion.'

'What?'

'You cannot really know what is going to happen next. But the mind creates an illusion of control: If I do this then this will happen. When it goes well, we assume that it was because we had the thought and we are in control.

'Ha! it is like we think we are driving the car but in reality we are sitting in the back with a child's little plastic steering wheel.'

A very large 'but' was on the tip on my tongue, but a mixture of having teed up my ball and not knowing what to say next helped me decide to delay my response to what seemed like utter nonsense. I also guessed that Mr Dog-with-a-bone would return to his theme. God knows why he had chosen me for the psychology and mysticism lesson. Or maybe it was the other way round: I'd chosen him!

The conversation set me thinking about my own experiences of meditation and creative visualisation, where the teachings involved harnessing the mind and creating the outcomes you desired. These teachings promised a great deal but were increasingly leaving me with a sense of frustration which his words about the illusion of control had tapped into. I guess they had helped in a minor way on the golf course but had never really helped me harness or control the mind. I'd often heard pro golfers talk about feeling 'in control' during a round. But once they'd achieved control why couldn't they manage to do this each time they played?

'So,' I wondered, 'if you'd mastered the mind why wouldn't this be permanent?'

'You can't "get" into the zone using control,' he explained. 'It is more like the zone finds you when the conditions are right, more of a being found than a finding or a grasping.'

My next shot, not surprisingly, proved this point.

My last two drives on this hole had been hooky and left. But this one was a big push off to the right. My shoulders slumped.

'Fear is a common occurrence when the mind and body remember recent outcomes and compensate by trying to exert more control,' he said, quietly.

I stood on the tee practising the swing, and muttering about why was it now going straight right after the other two disasters?

I should have realised that Big Ears was tuning in to my mutterings. Perish the thought that some part of me was seeking this out. That behind my irritation was perhaps a curiosity about what he would say next.

'The little ball did not go where you wanted it to go?'

'No, the little ball did not!'

'Ah... to desire is to suffer!'

What the **** does that mean? I thought. That flies in the face of what I'd been learning from my meditation teachings: 'Create what you want in life!'; 'Be the outcome you desire';

'The power is in your hands'. 'You can have everything you want': 'perfect health', 'enlightenment!'

This was all starting to feel a bit uncomfortable. I couldn't dismiss what he'd said outright. It spoke to a little voice of doubt that had been nagging in the background for years. The doubt and the evidence were right here on the golf course. Wanting to play well wasn't enough: feeling 'in control' wasn't really being in control. Focusing on the best outcome didn't really do it either.

The fourth hole is quite unique in appearance. To the left is a huge quarry-like crater running the length of the fairway. On the right is a steep bank that drops away about 50 feet parallel to the previous hole. With the quarry and the last two drives hooking left, in mind I had bailed out to the right and was down on the previous fairway. To stay on this fairway you have to drive the ball really straight as the target is narrow and the surface is hard, like trying to land your ball on your dining room table.

I started off down the slope, but the angle of the descent was a bit much for my trolley and it tipped over spilling half the contents of the bag – clubs, balls, tee pegs etc., into the rough grass. A few expletives later it occurred to me that this irritating event usually happened after a bad shot... and more obviously that it was less likely to happen on the generally flatter surfaces of the fairway.

At least my favourite ball marker that I'd been looking for was lying with the rest of the debris. What would his Taoist farmer say about that!

My ball was lying fairly well in the light semi-rough of the previous fairway but my shot to the green was blind. I didn't fancy running up to the top of the hill just to get a line and couldn't ask my companion. He was starting to point to a lot of things, but I doubted if he could grasp what I needed here.

The big slope was just in front of me. As so often happens when the hazard imposes itself on the mind, my swing was more of a shovelling motion than one that trusted the loft on the club face to do the job. It was enough to get the ball to the top of the slope but well short of the green.

I trudged up the slope after it puffing and muttering. I was well short of the green by some 60 yards but on some very short grass. Time for the Texas wedge, as it's called when you putt from off the green rather than chipping. The pin was another 20 yards from the front of the green, so a very long putt was required. I struck it well and on line. It seemed to travel for ages up to the hole, looking like it might end up close. It did travel close to the cup but carried on as though just passing through – another two, three, four and eventually six feet past.

The advantage of the ball having travelled past the hole was that I could see the route it took and was able to hit it back on that line… in it dropped… easy!

Putting is often described as a game within a game and this last hole was a good example. I'd hit two poor long shots but got down in two putts from 60 yards for a par! Spawning the other golfing expression 'it's not how but how many!' At the top of the game, when watching something like the Ryder Cup and the majors it's the putts that often make the difference; or as the Americans say 'You drive for show and you putt for dough.'

As I walked up a little slope to the next tee, I remembered

my new buddy's words about suffering... like a splinter that I'd forgotten about but one that was not going away. I had the distinct feeling we'd be returning to this theme before the round was over.

Chapter 5

The Fifth

I went to my room to be alone and decided to stop trying.
Ian Woosnam (after shooting 66 when needing to finish in
the top five to gain a Ryder Cup place)

The fifth tee is a grass island in a sea of gorse and sand. Beyond
the gorse the hole reveals only two features to the eye – a marker
post set on a postage stamp of a sharply sloping fairway, and
dog-legging to the right, a tiny flat green perched on a plateau.
In the distance a flat marshland stretches out with the sea
beyond creating the illusion of a green suspended in mid-air.

It is a daunting tee shot, anything right ends up in a hazard
resembling a quarry. Go left (even a ball hit with draw will
bounce sharply left off the fairway) and you are in the deep
heather, probably lost. Ideal is a low fade, landing against the
slope of the fairway and shaping towards the green.

My natural draw simply does not work on this hole and
many 'good' shots have ended in that beautiful but hungry
purple vegetation which for some reason, lost on golfers, is
associated with good luck. If you do bounce through the heather
then there's some yellow flowering vegetation waiting. And not
waiting in a benign way but ready to scratch any golfer foolish
enough to venture in to find or get his ball. Don't be fooled by
its sweet fragrance and pretty yellow flower.

The morning sun, still pale, was facing us and getting up
enough warmth to make the dew glisten and turn to mist,
adding a magical quality to an already wonderful hole. My
acquaintance was standing peacefully, breathing as though he
were breathing in the whole view.

I noticed I was already focused on how to play the hole

and his absence of interest in this and absorption in the air made an impact on me as though bringing me into balance. I automatically began breathing more deeply myself and noticed, as I did, that I felt a part of this view; not merely an observer but with a sense of belonging. What I was looking at appeared to be breathing too. After what seemed a very long time, I looked at him; he was smiling at me as though he knew what I was experiencing.

When I finally took my shot, I felt perfectly balanced as I set up and went through the swing. Only when I had completed the swing still in balance and very relaxed did I realise that I had not really thought about the shot I was playing. For a moment I was afraid and then amazed as I watched its flight: it started low down the left side of the fairway and then climbed into a steep fade and landing softly beyond the marker post and kicking like an off break up the hill and towards the green.

Golfers sometimes use the phrase 'that was one for the album' as though we could paste these beautiful shots into a collection. I certainly would have wanted to do that with this one. Although as soon as I thought this I realised the sheer impossibility of capturing more than one per cent of that experience. It was now gone forever. I thought of all those sporting nostalgia conversations that tried to recapture great shots or great goals. The good old days: marriages where people were trying to keep things as they were in the first flush of love; men and women desperate to keep their youth, our difficulty with death and consequently with living life to the full.

Reading my mind, my new friend told me the story of a man chased by a tiger. The man ran so fast that when he came to a cliff he could not stop and slipped over the edge. On his way down he grasped at a branch and hung there. The tiger looked down at him. As the man also looked down another tiger stood at the bottom of the cliff waiting for him. At this moment the man noticed just within his reach a single strawberry growing on the cliff face. He reached out, picked it and ate it.

'It tasted so sweet!' my friend said as though he could taste the strawberry.

'We only ever have this present moment!' he went on in case I hadn't got the point.

After this drive I was in a wonderful position for my second – about 130 yards to a flat table top of a green. The only real hazard was that you could roll off the green down a steep bank which protected the green on three sides. There is nothing behind the green apart from this drop and, half a mile or so on, the sea. Without the visual landmarks, getting the distance right is particularly challenging.

I had three quarters of a nine iron to the green. I decided that a full wedge would run the risk of flying too high and being affected by the wind. As can often happen when not taking the usual full swing, I steered the ball somewhat and I was lucky to remain on the putting surface some 30 feet from the hole. I speculated that I had fallen into my usual thinking pattern rather than the revolutionary method I was learning today. I was not even sure what I would call this other way of thinking. It was certainly trusting myself to rely on a form of intelligence that was available, but not graspable or fixable. Could I really trust my body to 'know' how to play the shot? Is that what had happened on the tee and before?

'Much of your time is spent not actually playing your game,' my companion from the East remarked.

He was noticing something that is a peculiar feature of golf that although a round can take between three to four hours, the time spent engaged in hitting the ball is less than two minutes.

'Zen masters of art spend many hours in contemplation of a blank canvas and the painting itself may take a few seconds,' he said.

'Yes, golf leaves a lot of time for thinking. Not sure I'd call it contemplation.'

'Or just walking,' he said.

Had I ever 'just' been walking on the course? Not thinking about the next shot or the last shot or something else in life, big or small, past or future?

'What do the painters think about in the hours before they paint?' I asked.

'They're not thinking!'

'What **are** they doing?'

'They're stilling the mind so that the creative can find them. The usual activities of mind don't leave enough space. The flute needs to be empty for the music to pass through.'

'But we need to be able to think to function in the world!'

'Yes, of course, but we then tend to use thinking for everything – the functional and the creative. Your game is a good example. Does it help to be thinking a lot in between your hits?'

'Well… er… actually, no it usually doesn't.'

'The thinking mind is useful for some sorts of knowing but for other types of knowing it is not and can even be a hindrance. It seems to be that your game mostly requires a different sort of knowing and that the thinking mind can get in the way of your connection to the playing?'

'Yes, often. Golfers often say you can overthink the game.'

'When you go swimming or ride a bicycle you do not think about how to do it each time. If you are able to swim and cycle they become natural to you, the body remembers. Is it not the same with your game of golf that once you can do the mechanics, thinking is not needed?'

'I suppose so.' I said, wondering why most golfers tend to treat the golf swing differently from swimming and cycling.

'The thinking mind divides things into parts,' he went on. 'Into subjects and objects. Useful in chess, architectural drawings or engineering, but your game is played out here in Nature, where there are no straight lines and everything is connected. No separate parts.'

He was on a roll now, his face lighting up and his words tumbling out.

'The thinking mind cannot see what is really there, the interconnectedness, the union of everything. The mind sees the sea and the shore, the grass and the earth, the land and the sky and all the other elements; and then itself, the me, as separate from all of this. As it says in your story of Adam and Eve as soon as they knew "I" there was separation from the Garden. Before they knew "I" they were part of the Garden, part of Nature, like our animal kingdom. Birds are not thinking, "I must sing better today." They are simply being birds, part of everything with no "I". In a way there is no bird singing. Just singing!'

At this moment, a gust of wind caught his jet black hair and sent it twirling upwards, bringing what looked like a slight nod of recognition, as though a friend had just called to him.

'So,' he continued, 'the Zen artist is hoping to go beyond the world of thought to the empty space into which everything flows; to lose his sense of "I" and be inspired by a world beyond himself.'

'I see!' I didn't really, but I did have a sense of what he was alluding to. All golfers know those shots where everything **felt** right, where the body seemed to know what was needed, where the swing felt easy and natural.

I told my companion of a time when I was practising putting on the carpet in our flat in Gloucestershire. I was using a rubber band as the hole and putting from around 15 feet. Anyone who has tried this knows that the pace of the ball needs to be perfect otherwise it simply rolls over the rubber band. In other words, it's extremely difficult!

My wife, a writer not a golfer, walked into the room and completely out of character said 'That looks easy... let's have a go.' It was only the second time in her life she'd held a golf club and the last time was a six iron!

I handed over the putter with a knowing smile.

However, first go she rolled the putt so that it approached the band as slowly as a Sunday driver and toppled gently inside it. Her triumph was fairly muted as, at that stage, she had no idea of what she had achieved and how difficult it really was.

I was in awe and incensed at the same time.

'I'll bet you a £100 that you can't do that again. And you can have a hundred goes!'

'Tell you what, instead I'll have those two lovely antique green wine glasses we saw earlier.'

'Okay it's a deal.'

She tried harder and harder with no success. The harder she tried the worse the result.

The glasses still managed to find their way to the dresser even though she'd lost the bet!

My friend piped up again.

'If there is no doer there is no one trying, just the pure activity.

'Ha! Ha! your wife has taught you an important lesson.'

'Yes, one of many!'

It reminds me of a woman who went to a monastery seeking enlightenment and asked the head monk how long this might take. The monk told her that this was hard to say but it could be 10 years or so. The woman then said 'Well, what if I try really hard and meditate four or five times a day?'

'Then it would take 20 years!' said the monk.

Certainly, effort has no place on the putting green, but can still creep into the mind's attempts to get the little ****** in the hole. Our conversation had raised the idea of trying and within that, the notion that there is a way of playing (and living) where activities just flow peacefully and easily.

My putt from the edge of the flat green was from 30 feet but not difficult and so any thoughts of 'trying' to get it close were not needed. The stroke was smooth and easy sending the ball gently rolling to a few inches from the cup.

Walking off the green I had a moment to really take in the view, which was a sea of gorse stretching out to the beach. Nature didn't seem to be trying.

Chapter 6

The Sixth

I think heroic deeds were all conceiv'd in the open air, and all free
poems also,
  I think I could stop here myself and do miracles.
Walt Whitman, 'Song of the Open Road', *Leaves of Grass*

The drive from the sixth tee is always testing and today, into a stiffish breeze, it was particularly so. With the conversation about 'trying' still bouncing around in my head I said to myself 'Don't try to hit it too hard.' My backswing was quite slow and relaxed but because of the breeze the background thought was to hit the ball harder. To try and force it into the wind. The result was a speedy jerky start to the downswing and a forward movement of the head. The shot result was a top, the ball being airborne for a second or two before disappearing into the long grass about 60 yards ahead.

'F****. That's what you get for trying to hit it too hard. Even though I'd had the thought not to.'

Every golfer knows the effect of this sort of trying and may even say to themselves there is no need to try and hit it harder. And every golfer knows that the thought can sneak up on you in the middle of the swing like a pantomime villain. Another example of how thinking can get in the way of a relaxed swing.

'The ball did not fly,' my companion said, pointing out what Basil Fawlty would call the 'bleeding obvious'.

'No, it didn't! I said through gritted teeth. 'Even though I had told myself not to try too hard.'

'The body does not hear "not".'

'What do you mean?'

'Try not to think of pink elephants.'

'Oh! Yes. I see what you mean.'

How many times had I said to myself 'don't go in the lake!' Or 'I don't want to be in that big bunker.' We can guess the rest.

Then how the hell do you navigate your way around a golf course where there are hazards on every hole? Although I did not say this out loud, he anticipated the question.

'We can simply notice and accept that this is what the mind does. No need to fight with this. The noticing itself creates some space between the thought and the observer of the thought.' He said.

'As the observer we see it as just a thought. If you can see it, you're not it.'

He was on another roll – good job there is a lot of walking in between shots in this game, I thought.

'Of course you are going to be aware of the hazards. That is normal. And even to start to think of the consequences. If this, or if that. Moving to the outcome. Concerned about the outcome. You cannot control the result. To think you can is an illusion.

My teacher was once asked to sum up all his teachings in one phrase; to which he replied "I don't care what happens." He didn't mean he did not care about life or other people. Simply that freedom was letting go of our investment in things turning out the way we want.'

'But I do care what happened!' I said, unable to disguise the whinging tone of a child whose ice cream had just dropped on to the pavement.

'Yes, of course. Notice and accept that too! And begin to practise wanting what you get rather than getting what you want.'

'Wow… I'll have to think about that!'

* * *

Because I'd not hit the ball very far there was less walking to do;

although I did a few minutes of walking around in circles in the long grass searching for my ball that had buried itself, hiding ashamedly as deep as it could go. Having found it, there was little choice but to take the sand iron and try to make as much contact as possible. For these shots in deep grass I remembered a tip that a guy called Steve passed on to me. He said to play the ball in the back of the stance and take the club up and bring it back down steeply. This minimised the amount of long tangly grass that the club head passes through. As usual, this worked quite well. The ball flew about 90 yards just reaching the fairway.

I resolved to play the next shot without caring what happened to it, which in a way felt counter to the whole reason for being out here. As fate would have it, I was now faced with the biggest bunker I'd ever seen on a golf course. It must be 40 foot in height on the side of a grassy hill. It is so big that it totally obscures the view of the green, which lies in a bowl surrounded by steep hills on three sides. If ever there was an 'in your face' hazard this was it! Many's the time I had allowed it to intimidate me; then, out of fear, tried to scoop the ball over it causing a dip in the swing and the club catching the ground before the ball; called a fat shot, in Spanish 'peso' (heavy).

The alternative, usually born of fear of the fat shot, is hitting it thin, the club head catching the ball half way up, sending it fast and low twice as far as intended except with this hazard where the result is the same. The ball from the fat shot loops slowly into that sand and from the thin crashes like a misguided missile into the face of the bunker. If you're lucky, the thin shot rolls down into the lower part of the bunker. If not, however, it is embedded in the slope – leaving the next shot for mountaineers only. Hence the bunker's nickname: Himalaya.

On the pink elephants theme my mind went through these scenarios and more all by itself! They were, of course, all about caring what happened to my ball and all sorts of outcomes. So, what would it be like to swing without caring? It certainly wasn't to do with blocking these thoughts out. They'd already arrived, sat down and made themselves at home. But perhaps I could accept they were there and that they were inevitable in any sport and particularly one with so much time for thinking. I could understand why one of the things I'd enjoyed about playing football was the lack of thinking time – just being in the flow of the game, responding intuitively to each situation. The only time this wasn't true was taking a penalty particularly in a penalty shoot out.

My golf ball still lay on the turf... waiting, impervious to all this inner chatter.

The backswing was fine, not a care in the world, but at the top of the swing came a slight tightening, a speeding up, and a little loss of balance. Thin. But not too thin. The ball just clearing the big bunker, giving the wispy grass on top a slight haircut. Okay, so it's possible to not care on the backswing and start caring when hitting the ball. Another lesson learnt. Another victory for the mind.

Also, my relief that the ball had cleared the bunker was a sure sign of caring.

When you walk around the huge bunker the green comes into view. It's set in a bowl surrounded by a bank on three sides. My ball had been straight but was not on the green, so must have been too low and fast to stop. Bound to be in the thick collar of grass all around the bank. This grass was thick and matted with long wispy bits. Because I'd not seen my ball go in, I could not be sure where to look... both the line and how far it had gone in. Sometimes you have to tread on the ball in grass this thick to find it; and I almost did, but just saw it before stamping it down any deeper. It was deep enough. Easy choice of club. Has to be the heaviest club in the bag, the sand iron. No real choice about how to play it either. Has to be a full swing – hit and hope. These shots are strange because, with a sand iron, a full swing usually means you're trying to hit the ball at least

90 yards. Here I'm hoping the ball pops out of the thick stuff and flies about three yards more like a bunker shot. I'm also standing with one leg a lot below the other on the slope.

'Oh well – here goes!' I thought to myself.

I made a full but easy swing which, in any other circumstance, would have sent the ball flying high and some distance. On this occasion the ball popped up slowly no higher than me and landed with a little thunk on the edge of the green. It finished 20 feet short of the pin but the result was fine and a lot better than the other possibilities.

Only after the shot did I think about the theme of not caring. Shots like this leave the mind no choice, no doubts. There is only one thing to do. Make a swing! All the interruptive swing thoughts disappear. No need for 'Is this the right club?', 'How hard do I need to hit this?', 'What if I don't hit it properly?' All the 'what ifs?' fall away.

It reminded me of an interview I'd heard with Jonny Wilkinson in which he had talked about the torture of his own what ifs? He said that if the referee had blown his whistle and stopped time just before he'd kicked the winning drop goal in the World Cup Final he would have been totally incapacitated by the thoughts of what could go wrong and the enormity of the situation, to the point where he would have curled up in a ball and started screaming.

Maybe these thoughts put my game into some perspective in terms of importance, but the putting stroke was relaxed and free and the ball rolled nicely at the hole straight in the middle but a little steamy. It hit the back of the hole and jumped up and sat rebelliously an inch on the far side of the cup.

A tap in for a 6.

Chapter 7

The Seventh

I just feel gratitude for being lent this talent.
Gary Player (April 2009, after his last US Masters)

The tee for the seventh is set back among some bushes and gorse so that the effect is of driving through a funnel. A drive off the heel disappears deep into the gorse at a proportional distance to its velocity – a fleeting thought that is best dealt with rather than acted out for real. A ball sent at pace in this direction rarely sees the light of day again.

The full length of the hole on the right is out of bounds. Bounded by a stone wall with a sea of dark green rushes beyond. Acres of marshland, with no respite from the rushes which, in a wind, swirl and sway as an eddying sea, and swish and whistle like a thousand reed pipes. The sight and sound are hypnotising and many a ball has curved an unerring path to its tentacles.

The hole itself is dead straight, over 400 yards and into the prevailing wind. A beast. The land falls away from left to right towards the out of bounds, dropping down about 80 feet. This flattens out at the narrow fairway, but with the reeds 'calling' aiming straight up the middle takes courage. The courage I thought I possessed deserted me on the downswing and turning the club over, I duck hooked. My ball span straight into the steep slope on the left as if it had run into a wall, coming to rest barely 160 yards from the tee.

I pointed out to my acquaintance the beauty of the marshland and because I was noticing his interest in the workings of the mind, I decided to tell him the contents of my head. I said I had allowed the thought of the marshes into my mind and it had affected my concentration.

'What is con-cen-tration?' he asked.

'It is keeping the focus of the mind on what you are doing.'

'Ah! I see,' he said, seeming genuinely pleased to have understood and really interested in my thoughts. In me, in fact! I noticed how refreshing this felt in contrast to many jaded conversations (golfing and others) in which people go through the motions, not wishing to learn anything or disturb the comfortable status quo.

'I think I know what you mean,' he went on.

'Recently, I left my room in a hurry to fetch something and left the windows to my room open. When I returned the wind had blown all my papers off my desk and scattered them all over the floor. The mind is like this sometimes, do you not think?'

'Yes,' I said, although it was a few moments before this image had made a full impact. When it did, not only did I think of golf and the countless times that I had allowed something to disturb my concentration and scatter my clear thoughts, but many other ideas were stimulated.

'When I'm playing, I'm trying to control my mind,' I said.

'Good luck!' he replied with a grin.

'What do you mean?'

'In Buddhism it's called "monkey mind", jumping from tree to tree. We won't control it, the most we can do is observe the mind and accept how it is.' he said.

'A lot of golfers and other sportsmen and women talk about being or feeling in control.'

'I don't know much about sport but I do hear many people say they are in control of their lives or want to be. This is an illusion! What do we really control in life? Do you know what will happen to you tomorrow? As we have just been saying, we cannot even control our thoughts!'

'But sometimes I feel in control.'

'I suspect these are times when you are in harmony with life, in the flow as it were. This creates the illusion that we are in charge of what's happening. Remember the child with its plastic steering wheel. We're really just fully part of what's unfolding. Just that ego thinks it's doing it all.'

'Do you mean I'm not doing it?'

'No, not really. More the opposite. When you get "you" out of the way you are more connected to the environment. The space between you and your target. The feel of your club in your hands. The strength of the wind in your favour or against you. The moisture in the atmosphere. The lie of the land. Do you imagine you are in control of these?' he asked me.

'Many years ago, an American president wrote to a Native American Indian chief asking to buy some of their land. The chief replied that he could try but wondered how he would own the hawk that flew across the mountain or the water that flowed through the river out to the sea.'

'So how do you get in the flow? I think what you're describing is what I've heard some sportsmen call being "in the zone".'

'Ha! There's a question. I think you call it a paradox? You cannot get in the flow because you are already part of the flow. You are flow! So, you can only be what you are by letting go of what you are not!'

'Derrrgh?'

'Take the notion of control, for example. If we let go of attempts to control life we will, quite spontaneously, be more in harmony with what occurs. Like our breathing. We don't need to control the breath. It comes and goes naturally. In fact, maybe like your game of golf, if we think about it too much, we interrupt the flow.'

We'd arrived at my ball. In fact, we'd got there a few minutes ago but the philosophy lecture was ongoing!

The little chap was lying fairly nicely in the semi-rough. The green was out of range but up a steep hill and round to the left between two hillocks. This next shot had to find the right position or the third would be blind and really difficult.

The 21-degree rescue felt like the right club and once again the previous conversation was permeating my mind even if I was far from really understanding what he was saying. The swing was easy, natural and flowing. There was a sweet clack of clubhead on ball and it soared off, landing in the middle of the fairway just over 200 yards away.

I looked over for his approval but he was engrossed in watching a kestrel hovering above its prey. Vigorous movements kept it perfectly still. The man's white shirt fluttered in the wind against the stillness of his body as he watched – almost mirroring the bird.

Walking to my ball I had a quiet sense of well-being. There was just someone walking in this beautiful landscape. Nothing needed to be added. It was all just fine as it was. Golf seemed incidental; but arriving at the ball the thoughts started to surface again. The difference this time was that the quiet sense of well-being was more foreground leaving the thoughts with less importance like clouds scudding across a clear blue sky.

I was faced with a shot of 100 yards or so up to the green between the humps. The stance and the wedge in my hands felt easy and I'd made the swing without too much thought and preparation. It flew high and straight, landing close to the pin, although I couldn't see how close as the green was up above my eyeline.

Was this the zone? I wondered. The question was a guaranteed way of leaving the zone if indeed I had been in it!

As we climbed the steep slope to the green, my ball came into view; it was on line with the hole but just past by four feet or so. I said to myself 'Just stay in the zone!' which is probably a bit like saying 'Be spontaneous!'

The result was me acting as though I was in the zone which, I soon discovered, is not the same as being there.

My pretence involved being super relaxed so that my putting stroke was a limp waft at the ball sending it only three of the four feet required.

I tapped in the remaining short putt feeling more confused than angry.

What did he say? 'Only by letting go.' So, you can't get in the zone, as this in itself involves a tension which is not the zone. Maybe it finds you when you let go of thoughts and tensions. No wonder I'm confused!

Chapter 8

The Eighth

It was the worst decision of my life to change my swing. I am now just swinging and playing by feel.
Gordon Brand Jnr.

The eighth hole is a par 5 – distance 487 yards. A brook runs from the left of the tee, crosses in front of the tee and runs the length of the hole on the right-hand side. For the tee shot, the closer you go to the brook the further down the fairway you can go. But if you go left for safety you can easily find a couple of little bunkers on the left-hand side.

My new companion picked up on my thoughts.

'You look a little concerned?'

'This is a difficult shot... quite intimidating!'

'Ah, the mind and its perceptions!'

'What do you mean?'

My companion related a story of a man who walks along a path and meets another man who says, 'What is the town like that you just came from?'

The first man replies, 'What is the town like that you have just left?'

'Terrible!' says the man, 'People were always fighting with each other, there was lots of jealousy, conflict and ill will.'

'The town I have just left is like that too,' says the first man.

In a short while he meets another man on the same path who also asks:

'Sir, what is the town like that you just came from?'

Again, the first man asks:

'What is the town like that you have just left?'

'Ah,' the man replies, 'Wonderful! There was much love and

kindness. The people were friendly and cooperative.'

'The town I have just left is like that too,' says the first man.

The little parable helped me realise that I had already filled the next shot with expectation, probably creating some tension and anticipation in the body. These little tensions tiptoe into the swing and will always cause an attempt to steer rather than trust, affecting the result which then confirms the original thought as to how difficult the shot was!

He carried on:

'It is like we all wear our own unique tinted spectacles which bring our perception of the world to each experience. Your game is a good example of this... Of course these perceptions can influence a whole life!'

'Can we get rid of these perceptions?'

'Not really and anyway there's no need. The problem is not that we have our own view of things but that we take this to be real and identify with it. It's simply a question of knowing what our own spectacles are like and observing how they influence clear perception. Just notice how you impose your personal view of reality... what follows is a spontaneous letting go.'

Just noticing these thoughts and the sensations seemed to help. I remembered something I'd read about quantum physics: as soon as an object is observed it is changed.

* * *

By the time I stood over the drive the thoughts and perceptions of the hole were still present but now more distant. It enabled me to stay relaxed through the swing without the expectations running the show. Relaxed in this way, the timing was good, the ball flew off the middle of the club face and sailed down the middle of the fairway. Now the shot didn't seem so difficult!

As we walked along the fairway, I noticed that he walked slowly but powerfully as though all the energy in his body were engaged in the process.

'Do you play a sport or exercise in some way?' I asked.

'No, not a sport but I practise yoga.'

'What type of yoga?' I said, as if I was an expert.

'Hatha yoga is the name of the formal practice.'

'Formal,' I thought, prompting the immediate image of him being upside down in a tuxedo. I quickly asked a sensible question, which distracted me from a chuckle.

'Formal?'

'Yes, the regular practice of breathing while holding the body in certain positions. But really all of life is yoga,' he said.

'Really?'

'Yes, yoga means union. The formal practice is just a reminder of the union between our bodies and the space around us, the earth on which we stand. The marriage of stillness and movement. Like the world spinning on its axis. Without the still point there could be no spinning. Your game of golf is yoga!'

* * *

We had arrived at my ball by this point, which was probably a good thing as I was feeling a little out of my depth.

Even so I couldn't help noticing my breath as I took the practice swing with the 3 wood I'd chosen for the task in hand. The breath came in on the backswing and out on the downswing. Was that always true? Or just today? Or just with a 3 wood? Or only when playing in the company of yoga teachers?

Whatever the case, I was aware of the breath during the actual swing too. Same again. The effortless nature of the breath seemed to make for a swing without effort; but one where that effortless energy flowed through the body and club, meeting the ball with an added intensity. It flew, low at first and then climbed into the blue sky, hovered for a while, seemingly motionless, before finally dropping into a bunker that I'd estimated was well out of range.

We walked in silence down to the bunker near the green but I imagined I could feel us walking and breathing in the same rhythm. My ball was too far into the bunker to get any distance so I only managed to splash it out 20 yards short of the green. I now had a simple pitch and run to the pin. But even though I'd been playing this wonderful/tortuous game for decades, I once again succumbed to the most basic of errors. On the downswing I became eager to see the result before playing the shot. This rarely works out well. On this occasion the club made no contact with the ground but caught the ball about half way up. It scooted past the pin and disappeared off the back of the green and half way down a steep bank.

Golf again the winner. Two great shots to near the green on a par five and now struggling to make 6... Grrrh.

Having suffered the head up on the last shot, the memory focuses the mind for the next one and so was determined to watch the ball at impact and trust the swing. The contact was good and the ball popped up, landed softly on the green and trickled down to the hole. A tap in 6 leaving a mixture of feelings. Nothing new there then!

Chapter 9

The Ninth

At the still point of the turning world.
T.S. Eliot, 'Burnt Norton', *Four Quartets*

A seaside links is usually a strip of land that runs parallel to the seashore, the golf course heading out in one direction and back in another. It means that the wind direction might be against the player for the first nine and with you on the way back or vice versa.

The ninth is a short hole that turns away from the sea and starts the return to the clubhouse. This part of the course is often called 'the turn'.

This phrase is also used to describe an aspect of the golf swing. The whole body turning away from the ball and then returning in the downswing, through impact with the ball and then completing the turn in the follow through. Not completing the turn on the backswing results in poor timing.

This was exactly what happened in my swing of the seven iron that I took to this short hole. The result was to hit it 'fat'. As some golfers say, 'I hit the big ball first'. The club strikes the earth before the ball taking distance off its flight. The amount of distance lost depends on how much of the earth you catch before the ball. In this instance it wasn't much, but enough to cause it to find the huge bunker that protects the front of the green.

Some bunkers on links courses are completely different from parkland courses. Some are so deep that steps are built in so you can climb in there, and then so deep you can only see the face of the bunker and nothing else. This was such a hazard. You might be inclined to admire the symmetrical wooden rivets in the face that prevent the grass and sand collapsing, but rarely is the golfer in the mood for sightseeing if standing in one of these (sand) pits of despair. The lie is all-important and my ball wasn't so much lying as hiding – two thirds of it below the creamy-coloured powdery sand.

A friend had recently told me that the secret to playing the plugged lies is to aim to hit the ball with the toe of the club. It didn't seem logical to me but, what the hell, the shot looked impossible anyway!

I did manage to make contact with the ball. To my amazement it popped up and out of the bunker – but not very far, and only onto the top of the bunker. It then rolled sideways for a couple of feet before rolling backwards down the slope at the side of the bunker. I was out but 20 yards further away from the hole!

The grass was cut short where my ball lay and normally I would have putted from off the green. However the edge on the bunker was between my ball and the flag so I had no choice but to chip. The conversation we'd had about the still point had dripped into my consciousness and the swing felt like a perfect turn on the still axis, with the stillness somehow infusing the quality of the turn.

'There is an inherent stillness in Nature,' my friend said. 'Not a literal stillness but something more fundamental... you can see it in a bird in flight or the swaying of a tree in the breeze.'

I started to wonder how this applied to a golf swing. It reminded me of watching the true champions live when I'd been to pro tournaments: Player, Nicklaus, Ballesteros, Watson. There was a sort of stillness about their presence on the course. For them, this stillness was almost constant, but for the mere mortal golfer has just an occasional glimpse, if you're lucky.

Their swings involved a full turn of the body but around a still centre and a stillness of being.

'How do we find that stillness?' I asked.

'You cannot find it!'

'Why?'

'Because you are it! Every step to find it is a step away from it. Searching is restlessness not stillness. Simply stop! And be true to who you are!'

'I don't understand,' I said.

'It can't be grasped, only deeply known.'

That was a conversation stopper! All my other questions arose and fell into a pit of despair.

As if sensing this, he told a story:

'My five-year-old nephew had some friends round to play and shared some apple juice with them. Being a good host, my nephew poured his friends' drinks first and his last. His drink had all the sediment and was cloudy.

'"What shall I do, uncle?" he asked.

'I told him to go and play and come back in a while. When he did the juice was clear, with all the sediment in the bottom of the glass.

'My nephew was very pleased and excited and said, "It's all clear! Has it been meditating like you?"'

I had been meditating for many years but in a system that encouraged progress and a disciplined search for enlightenment. The notion of meditation as stopping was radical for me! Surely it couldn't be that simple? What about all those years of following a path with the promise of the holy grail at the end? Perseverance was supposed to be the answer. If the mantra was repeated enough times the goal would be achieved. That none of this might be necessary was shocking.

'All those years that I was meditating. Are you saying they were a complete waste of time?'

'No,' he smiled. 'Although there is no path to take, we need to take a path to know this! Meditating in this way is searching, desiring and grasping. It takes us away from stillness. You cannot get to what you already are. But we need to experience this to know it. As though we are standing on a platform as a train goes past at 90 miles an hour. It is because we are still that we know the speed of its movement.'

'But...' I began as I turned round to continue the conversation. Instead of being next to me he'd stopped and was crouching down yards away, staring at a small wild orchid.

I wasn't sure what the rest of my sentence was going to be anyway, so was left with his infuriating and yet intriguing ideas messing with my mind.

* * *

Anyway, it was time to play my next shot.

My chip over the bunker had ended up four feet from the hole, but above it, leaving a fast downhill putt with some borrow – a putt where you have to get the pace and the line right to have any chance of holing out. The whole notion of stillness was still with me and I made a pretty good stroke but the ball horseshoed in and out and around the hole finishing up at the front door having tried the back door and both sides. It almost toppled back in but stayed teetering on the edge. A golfer is allowed to wait a few seconds in case the ball loses its balance and falls in but this is rare. So, the golfer is left with the shortest shot in golf which counts as one hit as much as a drive of 270 yards.

* * *

Half way round. Time for a snack. I reached into the bag for the flapjack I'd hastily thrown in before leaving. I pulled it out, only to realise this was the same flapjack I'd put in the bag at least a month ago. It was easy to tell the difference because the yoghurt coating was no longer on the flapjack but part of the plastic cover.

I found today's, broke it in half and offered one half to my companion.

'No, thank you very much. I am fasting.'

'Oh, okay. Why are you doing that?' I said, thinking 'this is the turn maybe I get to ask the questions now!'

'There are many reasons but mostly I enjoy the freedom it brings.'

'Freedom? I thought it would bring the opposite.'

'I'm sorry to say that in Western culture you misunderstand freedom. You imagine that freedom is doing what you like, going where you want, buying what you want, eating when and what you like. It is why in the West you struggled to let go of these "freedoms" during the pandemic.'

'That's true,' I said, 'but I also spoke to many people who enjoyed the simplicity of being locked down in their homes, excluding those in high rise flats or in violent relationships, of course.'

'Yes, we were deprived but free from wanting... an enforced retreat into a sort of monastic life.'

Chapter 10

The Tenth

Potential employer: 'What are you good at?'
Siddhartha: 'I am good at waiting.'
Herman Hesse, *Siddhartha*

As we arrived on the tenth tee, I could see the fourball ambling down the tenth fairway. They had started on this hole, which they had every right to do. Also, they could not have seen us sitting on the bench by the ninth green.

I felt a strong irritation, I had played the first nine in an hour and a quarter and had enjoyed the pace. These guys could slow me up for at least a hole or two.

Normally I would have had a golfing partner to grumble about this with. I was about to invite my companion to join me in my complaint but when I looked around, he was sitting on a mound of grass looking out to sea. Time did not seem to matter to him and his face was a picture of serenity. Looking at him, the little knot in my stomach dissolved instantly. I followed his gaze and could not believe that I had not even noticed the magnificent view that lay before us.

'Come and sit,' he said softly, but not seeming to offer a choice. We sat for about five minutes in silence. I only realised later that he was inviting me to join him in his style of meditation. I had been used to meditation with a goal, trying to achieve something, get somewhere, find peace. 'Doing' meditation, repeating a mantra, visualising outcomes.

This sitting was so simple and ordinary. Gulls glided across the sky, the longer grass swayed in the wind, the molten grey-blue sea glistened in the sunlight. Everything was simply being itself. And in these moments so was I. Just sit. Not even breathing was 'doing'. The breath came naturally breathing me rather than me doing anything. All this left me with a deep sense of stopping, of simply being, of life just as it is and of the stillness at the heart of it all.

A sense of time was completely lost. We could have been sitting there for seconds or hours.

* * *

The tenth runs 390 yards all the way down hill, falling at least 100 feet. Only 80 yards behind, the green huge white topped breakers crashed on to the shingle so powerfully that we could hear them easily from where we were. The coastline stretched out before us for miles in each direction. The breeze was strong here, clearing all the cobwebs from the mind and body.

I thought about waiting. Those breakers rolled in from the immense sea, reached their crests and seemed to 'wait' for a second before surrendering themselves to the glistening pebbles and breaking into foam.

I remembered choosing some cashew nuts in a tiny shop in India with a friend. The shop which stood on the corner of a busy street, only sold cashew nuts. The four staff, who barely had room to move behind the counter – all men, all middle aged – looked military in their style and demeanour. The senior member sported a huge handlebar moustache and was clearly the 'colonel'. The walls of the shop had rows of proud photographs of Nehru, Gandhi and Ganesh covering the fading, peeling paint. It could have been any point in time in the last hundred years.

My friend explained that he did not want the nuts with the skins that he had had before, as they had taken so long to peel. The colonel grinned a huge grin and simply said, 'Ah... waiting is wonderful!'

His comment stayed with me for a long time and challenged

all my rushing around, eating fast food fast, going from place to place, person to person, without time for reflection. Not long afterwards, back at work, I stood cursing a door that was taking too long to close. Our fire doors had been adjusted, because they had been making a loud bang as they closed automatically. Now they took 20 seconds or so to close before we could lock them. It was in these 20 seconds that I found myself berating the door because my busy life would not allow for this delay. Fortunately, the words of the cashew nut colonel broke through my temporary insanity.

As I stood on the tee, I thought of my father held up on the golf course or in a traffic jam, steam coming out of his ears as he was forced to wait; of my own impatience and dislike of waiting. Even my swing showed evidence of this, my worst shots occurring when I did not wait to complete my backswing and started down to soon.

Something about the sea within earshot, the memory of India and the simple sitting I had just experienced helped with this thought. The timeless unhurried pulse of the waves on the shore became a rhythm that moved through me. My swing on the drive was like a wave rising, pausing and crashing through with power. My timing was perfect; the ball flew low and straight and climbing at the end of its path.

'Beautiful!' said my companion.

I thought he meant my shot until I saw he was still looking at the view. As I looked at him it seemed to me that he was not simply looking at the view but rather absorbing it through each cell in his body, breathing in the whole experience. Watching him began to have a curious effect on me. It was like the edges of things began to dissolve. This was no longer man on seat looks out to sea but more man/grass/sky/sea all rolled into one. I swear that someone said the word 'one' at this moment but neither of us did. I felt a moment of simple bliss.

Time also became distorted as I looked. I don't know how

long we were there. It was also as though nothing else mattered. If the players in front had not called to attract my attention to call me through, we might have been there for ages. They had lost a ball in the deep rough to the right and were waving and, by now, calling me on.

We set off in silence, the memories of that experience still tangible for me but also frustratingly distant.

It is a very steep descent to the fairway and I was half jogging in order to get through the fourball. My ball was on the short grass, but on a steep downhill lie. I reckoned on a seven iron to the green.

By this time all my composure from the tee was gone. I hurried my setup routine, did not think through the shot and came up too quickly on the swing. The result was a squirty, low, thinnish shot heading off 20 yards right of the green. Two bounces right off the slope and the ball came to rest in a little swale some 40 yards right of the green and probably 30 feet below it.

I berated myself silently for allowing myself to be put off by a classic golfing distraction. When being let through it is easy to change your normal rhythm of play and then think and swing differently. I also felt that I had cheated myself of that special sensation of sending the ball flying high to a green lying well below me, especially this green. A well struck short iron climbs into the sky, hangs over the sea for ages and at best lands softly on the green.

The ball flying at the target seems to satisfy a primitive urge in man; perhaps a dim memory of the hunt. I only know the exhilaration I feel while the ball is in mid-flight, holding my breath as it hovers over the target or urging it on, encouraging it 'get up' or 'sit down' or as an American would say, 'be right!', depending on the flight in relation to the green. Sometimes, on a new course or in a wind, the ball lands well short or flies clean over the putting surface. At other times the ball lands on the target and every golfer knows the feeling of this result, justifying club selection, a good swing and a crisp strike. This experience is even better if you are watching in the balanced pose of a full follow-through.

I have played with people who have hit only one shot like this in a round. The rest have all gone along the ground; some only a few feet. Yet we are all back the following week as though that shot were enough to keep us interested. Enough to feed our addiction.

My wave of thanks to the players letting me through was contaminated by my ongoing grumpiness about the last shot. They were too engrossed in their task to notice. They were tramping in random circles in grass so long that it might have as easily yielded small mammals as golf balls. Each was walking in the manner that suggested the only real hope of finding the errant sphere was to stand on the thing. Much of golf is absurd and this scene was no exception.

As we proceeded downhill towards the green, I began to smell the sea – salty and musty seaweed. The sound of the breakers was much louder and I thought if I listened carefully, I could identify each pebble as each wave drew powerfully back into the mass of water. I remembered that I had read somewhere that the people of New Guinea did not have a noun for the word wave, they used a verb meaning 'waving'. It made sense to me at this moment. Our language can be very static. Also, what is the breaker without the beach? My thoughts wandered on: golfer/ball/flight/green. Perhaps those exhilarating seconds are glimpses of the unity of everything. Me in harmony with the club, the ball, the flight, the wind, the green. Is that what we are addicted to? Do we seek to be fully part of everything again? Before I, the human being, knew I was me, a separate entity, did I exist as an animal, primitive but at one with my environment?

With these thoughts still in my mind, I arrived at my ball. It was lying well in light rough. In front of me was a steep bunker and beyond that, twenty feet further on, the pin. Behind the green was a grass bank of 12 feet or so in height. I was well below the green. The beach is only a stone's throw away. I can see large bleached pieces of driftwood lying where the wet sand meets the dry. The water on the wet sand was almost too bright to look at with the sun reflected in it.

Perhaps because of my experiences sitting with my companion earlier, I was reminded that these feel shots are very much to do with my connection with my environment. At this point, the golfer is not thinking, 'I will take the club back three feet four inches and then bring it through at a speed of 65 mph in order to fly the ball the right distance'. Instead they are getting some feel for the distance in the hands and body. Hoping to allow the 'intelligence' in my body to 'know' what to do.

I thought, this is the type of knowing that my new friend has been talking to me about – the body relating to its surroundings and the relationship of aspects of these surroundings to each other. Body to ground. Body to club. Club to ground. Club to ball. Ball to ground. Ball to wind. Ground to sky and so on. More to do with our connection to the world around us rather than any technical achievement.

I was excited about this thought and made a good easy swing at the ball. However, I got too excited and looked up too soon to admire the result. The result was more of a scoot than a floated flight. Fortunately the ball hit the bank behind the pin and all its momentum was stunned. It trickled back haplessly into the rough fringe on the edge of the green. Once again, I had not waited to complete the shot and I had one of those 'How many times do you have to learn this?' conversations inside my head.

I saw my companion was now walking on the beach and at this moment agreed with whoever said that 'golf is a good walk spoiled!'

He had his sandals in one hand and his feet almost lingered on the hard wet sand with each step. The wind filled his white shirt, flapped his trousers and stretched the roots of his hair. He looked tiny on the expanse of beach, but solid, like a little sailboat steering a course through an ocean.

I realised through this temporary absence how important it had become for me to have him with me. I felt a little lost without his presence, although this was difficult to define. It wasn't just the content of his words and ideas, or even the fresh perspective that he was introducing me to, but something about his being.

I trudged up the steep slope to the green, along a little path between the bunkers. I was fairly puffing by the time I reached the top and the wind gusted over the unprotected surface of the green knocking me off balance slightly.

My ball was lying barely 20 feet from the pin but hard up against the thick fringe of thicker grass. Any attempt to get the putter face on the ball would be problematic and only the top third of the ball was above the fringe. I had seen some of the pros use the blade of the sand wedge in this sort of spot. I had never played this shot or even practised it but decided to give it a whirl.

It made sense to grip the wedge really short and make a putter swing, hoping to meet the ball with the flange end of it. Perhaps as a result of the extra concentration I employed because of the newness of this shot, I made a really smooth swing and a good contact. The ball climbed the little hill just in front of it and headed off in a determined way towards the hole. Had it not hit the pin square on and dropped like a stone into the cup it would have finished at least four feet past.

The instant the ball disappeared, a mop of jet black hair appeared at the level of the far end of the green. This, in turn, was closely but slowly followed by a rich brown face. Gradually his whole body came into view as he negotiated the steep slope up to the green. His progress was clearly not enhanced by the sandals he was wearing and he was concentrating hard to keep his grip and balance. His expression as he climbed was more serious than at any other time in our round. But when he reached the top he beamed with his achievement. I was, in a rather solitary way, still enjoying mine so we smiled at each other and walked in silence to the next tee.

When he arrived at tee he said, 'Thank you for waiting.'

Hardly noticing the coincidence, I said that I had been thinking about waiting, and particularly in relation to the golf swing. I don't know why I expected him to be interested in it, but to my surprise he launched into another little speech.

'Waiting is not something we can try and do. It's more of a letting go, more like allowing a space. It emerges in our stillness. It's the same when people meditate and have a blissful experience and then try to recreate it. You cannot recreate a natural wait in your swing because as soon as you are trying you are not waiting anymore. True waiting is acceptance which naturally dissolves any resistance. You can't create a space. The space is already there and finds us when we are open and ready.'

Chapter 11

The Eleventh

If I wasn't a professional, I would not play this game if you paid me.

Christy O'Connor

'Who taught you this game?'

'My father. He was called Jack.'

'I'm called Ram – by the way.'

'Oh, thank you – I'm Martin.'

'What did your father want for you?'

His questions usually went to the heart of the matter and were quite shocking to my defences. In another way I welcomed his directness, it took me to the centre of things.

'My father wanted me to love the game he loved and to be a professional.'

'What is being a professional?'

'To play golf for a living.'

'Ah! And you did not want this?'

For many years I had told myself that I had wanted this and had not been good enough. Now as I looked back on the path I chose, I don't think that I did really want that way of life. Instead I feel good about what I have found.

'For years, in my late teens and early twenties, I thought I did want to be a professional but this changed.'

'It is important for a man to find his own way and for his father to let him. The father must also bury his own dreams with a clear heart.'

'Yes, I agree,' I said, although more out of politeness than an appreciation of the true significance of what he was saying.

Having said this, I felt how strongly golf had connected my

dad and me. He was 45 when I was born and 63 when I was 18. Almost two generations separated us and when the Beatles and the Rolling Stones appeared on *Top of the Pops* and became my heroes it was like a million generations separated us. Add to that our political views and not much was left to talk about. Golf and other sports were our saviours.

We would stand in the bar at the golf club. All his friends wore crusty old sports jackets and quietly and not so quietly supported Enoch Powell. Aged 18, I had hair down to my shoulders and already thought of myself as closer to communism than anything else. Had I not represented the club at county level, I would probably have been forcibly ejected from the building. And Dad would have helped!

But I knew he was proud of me. Our love could be expressed on the links, in the admiration of each other's shots, in the joy of the competition and in the sharing of the sheer pleasure of the game. It made me wonder why we men seem so scared of true intimacy? Perhaps had he been more able to openly express his love for me then I might not have strived so hard to please him on the course. I had a momentary yearning for unconditional love. This led to a fantasy of me missing an important putt and of him putting his arm around me and saying 'It's okay, I still love you.'

My game had improved since letting go of my father's expectations and beginning to 'play my own game'. But I started to feel sad that he was no longer alive and that I could not discuss these reflections with him on the great game we love, man to man.

There were many possibilities for his difficulties in expressing love. His father, a master tailor, was largely absent in his life and his mother, who was Swedish, was cold, bitter and unhappy. Dad had also fought in the Second World War and lost many comrades in the conflict. He returned from the war to England with his German bride, my mum, and no doubt lost friends this way too. He was not allowed to continue a career in the Army, having married the 'enemy'.

I thought of his father who he barely knew, long dead before my birth and not spoken of. We rarely talked about such things anyway, but my grandfather was an alcoholic, left many debts and had a poor reputation in the family. Only many years later, soon after my father's death, did I see things in a different light when organising my father's resting place. My mother and I chanced upon the long-lost family gravestones. Overgrown, the stones all at different angles, the little collection of graves told a story pieced together with our assumptions. My grandfather had lost three of his siblings in the space of two years and had buried two wives in their 20s before he was 30. Perhaps the alcohol was his medication.

Did he make little or no attachment to my father having lost too many loved ones? Was it his legacy to my dad and me?

My first memories of walking round the course with Dad, when I was probably about nine or ten, were of what he wore and the way he played. In those days he wore plus fours (trousers that stopped and were buckled just below the knee) with long diamond-patterned socks. He used to wear a shirt and tie on the course too.

I remember his swing – graceful and effortless, yet powerful, the ball usually soaring into the sky. There was no fuss, no practice swing, no lining up, no calculating the distance with fancy electronic devices. He played quickly really well... being a scratch golfer for many of his younger years. Before the war, in the summer months, he and a friend would often play four rounds in one day!

'Did he fulfil his dreams?' asked Ram.

'No, I don't think so,' I said, more intuitively than having thought this through.

'He found love with my mum but was not happy in his career... I think he felt trapped but gave up a lot to support us financially.'

But as I thought about it in that moment, perhaps his swing portrayed something else? His golf swing suggested freedom, grace and power. The way he played seemed to show his deep love and connection to the course and the environment. Little of this seemed to be openly expressed in his daily life.

* * *

Perhaps because of what I was being exposed to on the course today, I started musing on these ideas more deeply. What if the game and the golf swing give us an opportunity to get more in touch with a natural self? What if life is essentially graceful and free and our thinking minds and personal prisons get in the way. What if the game challenges us to come back to Nature, and in so doing our true Nature?

Perhaps my father's swing (and maybe all our swings at times) gave a glimpse of his true Nature, before all the personal traumas and doubts had crystallised so firmly that they seemed to be who he was. This thought made me tearful but fortunately the wind was strong enough that I could disguise this as a watery eye. Or so I thought!

'I'm sorry if I have upset you asking about your father.'

I decided not to hide what I was feeling.

'No need to apologise. I was just realising what I missed about him.'

I'd never really looked into Ram's eyes but now I did and seemed to see them as smiling even though he wasn't actually smiling. His eyelids closed once very slowly and opened again as though clearing a screen of all its contents.

I was certainly seeing my father more clearly.

Looking into Ram's eyes reminded me of passing an exam in Zurich several years after Dad's death. I bought myself a little celebratory gift at the airport – the new Eric Clapton album. I settled into my seat and played the first track on my CD player: 'My Father's Eyes' thumped through the headphones reducing me to tears so prolific that the woman next to me asked if I was okay.

How important it is for us to share these successes with our fathers.

* * *

The eleventh hole is a remarkable short hole: 150 yards from one part of a cliff to another, playing over the beach. I stood on the tee with the spirit of my father alive in my body. I did not seem interested in lining up the shot, practising the swing or any sort or preparation. I simply waggled the club a little, stood to the ball and swung. There was a freedom of movement that you might see in a dolphin or a cheetah. It felt like no effort at all was involved and yet the club head met the ball, followed by the turf and the ball sailed off into the morning sunshine, rising all the way, hanging in the sky for what seemed like an age before finally dropping on to the green some 20 feet from the pin. The word 'shot' came from somewhere in my head to which I silently replied 'thank you.'

Although I enjoyed the shot, the walk along the gravel path round the cliff edge to the green was poignant and sad. More tears came but weren't just sadness but a mixture of grief and gratitude. I felt thankful initially to Dad and then to golf and then to the course and finally to Nature itself. This game had given me a window into his true Nature – and now into mine.

'Thank you,' said Ram as we got to the green, 'for letting me join you today. This is very beautiful.'

We stood on the green for a few moments, the sea stretching out to the horizon on one side, the beach below us and the tee tucked in the cliff from where we'd come. This was the most exposed part of the course and the wind bent the pin and fluttered the flag vigorously. I could only just stand still over my putt and my eyes were watering for all sorts of reasons. The wind held my putt up and, although on line it stopped a few inches short. I tapped in for a par.

As I walked off the green and up the steps to the next tee it was as though everything was filled with gratitude: my feet on the earth, the sun on my skin, the screech of the gulls, the smell of the sea and the grass in the wind.

Chapter 12

The Twelfth

It is essential movement without interference from the mind, arising naturally from the body's need to function in harmony with its environment. Action is the normal attitude of a being in tune with his own energy and with the energy of the planet.
Oscar Ichazo (unpublished)

We walked to the next tee in silence for a minute or two and then Ram asked:

'Do others in your family play golf?'

'Yes, I was supposed to play with my brother today but he's not well. He must be really poorly as he's even more of an addict than me and loves being out on the links.

'My mum used to play too. When she came to this country in 1947 from Germany she'd never even heard of golf! She was athletic though, having thrown the javelin as a youngster. She's now on her 97th hole on the great course of life.

'My dad introduced her to golf and generally to English culture. I think she had a tough time in those early days. There was a lot of prejudice.'

'Ah the human mind... what suffering it causes.'

I didn't ask any more but imagined that he had personal experience of racial prejudice.

* * *

Although the pressure is not as strong these days, trying to play well to please my father has been like a lover pulling the petals off a daisy. Good shot – he loves me, bad shot – he loves me not. If I played well, I felt good about myself not just as a golfer but as a person. If I played badly, I was simply not good enough as a golfer and, deep down, as a person.

My self-esteem was on a roller coaster of confidence and self-doubt totally dependent on results. Maybe that was why I turned to football for many years. At least if I wasn't playing well, I could try harder, run more, tackle harder, be part of the team's success. Being dropped from the first team did not feel good though!

Golf was more exposing. The ball was stationary. No one else was involved and the results immediate and obvious for all to see. A wild swing, nearly missing the ball completely and sending the ball bobbling along for only a few yards is very embarrassing and even brings one's masculinity into question.

People secure in their own identity and with less riding on the outcomes can laugh these shots off and move on. Those of us with deeper wounds to our self-esteem feel these poor shots as confirmations of what we knew already.

I was ready to initiate a question myself.

'What makes you happy, Ram?'

'Nothing makes me happy,' he replied.

Because of his accent and use of English, I wasn't sure what he meant.

'You mean nothing?'

'No, I mean no thing. In the West you live in a world of things. You imagine the next new shiny thing will make you happy. It does for a few minutes. You even treat each other like things. This wife that used to make me happy now makes me unhappy. I'll get a new one!

'True happiness is non-attachment!'

'Isn't that cutting off from everything?'

'No, that's detachment. In your culture you are often overly attached or detached. Here we are talking about recognising our attachments but without grasping, clinging or avoiding. You can see it in your game. You suffer if you are overly attached to the outcome. But if you were completely detached you would not even get out of bed to come here!'

'So how do you get to that state of mind?'

'There's the catch! As soon as you are trying to get somewhere you are back in the realm of attachment. As soon as we begin to notice our attachments, we are brought home to non-attachment.'

'How does that work?'

'There is a contrast. If our mouths were made of salt, we could not taste salt. Attachment is observed by the non-attached aspect of our being. The silent witness.'

'So, it's not a problem that I care about the outcome?'

'No, just notice and fully accept how much you care about what happens.'

'And then think that it's not really that important.'

'More thinking will not work. The mind cannot solve problems of its own making. In observing we simply take a sort of step back from the mind, a step back from all the chatter into the silent witness.

'There is a neutrality there as in Nature. Nature doesn't care if the baby seal gets eaten by the killer whale or gets away but notice how perfectly everything has a balance. Nature is even reminding us that globally we humans are getting out of balance. You could say the pandemic has brought this into sharp focus.'

There was something about his use of the word balance that filtered through like coffee percolating. He was teaching about a different way of knowing and trusting that way too. In the past my mind would have settled on the idea of balance and tried to use it to make a better swing. I guess this was the grasping that he was talking about as well as the limitations of the mind.

Also, this way of thinking meant this was something I was trying to achieve, something to acquire. As he had said already, present in Nature and my Nature.

I started to wonder about balance in other aspects of my life too. This was like dropping a match into a box of fireworks. So many thoughts came. I decided to shelve them for another day but felt this was a rich source of enquiry.

* * *

The twelfth hole is a 400-yard par four running left to right in a dog leg. Bunkers make the tee shot narrow and the green is guarded by bunkers on the right, a pond on the left and out of bounds on the beach at the back. There is a mound at the front of the green too. Beyond the green is the Firth, today sparkling in the sunlight.

The talk of balance was still resonating although not at the forefront of my mind. I was more surveying the shot and wondering whether the fairway bunkers were in range with the breeze slightly against. I decided it was unlikely unless I hit my Sunday best.

It would have been fair to describe the swing with the driver as balanced and the ball set off low and bored into the wind without being too affected by it. The ball headed unerringly for the bunkers, two bounces later hopped merrily into the left-hand pot bunker of the two. Shot gone. There's no way to get anywhere near the green out of there. I was aware of the usual irritation but as I watched the feeling it sort of dissolved, like a wave falling back into the ocean.

We walked in silence along the fairway towards my ball lying in the bunker, which could only be seen standing next to the deep hazard. What could also be seen from this point was the green in the distance with the Firth behind it and beyond that the mountains in the haze.

It would have been an inviting second shot had I not had to climb down into the little pot bunker gripping a sand iron. Balance was an issue in there too as I had to stand with one foot in the sand and one on the rim of the bunker. Easy to fall over or even into the sand. I managed to keep my balance during the swing and popped the ball up into the air and 30 yards down the fairway.

The grass on links fairways is usually very short, requiring a precise contact with the ball. On this occasion my ball had run into a little gully in which some lush green grass had grown, making the shot a little easier. I decided on a soft nine iron for the next shot. The swing was easy and the ball flew high and straight. The hills and shoreline provided a backdrop for the flight of the ball and it hung in the air as though in a painting. For a moment everything seemed to have stopped as the ball hovered above the green. When it finally fell it landed about 20 feet left of the hole and took a small hop forward.

We walked silently into the painting as though not wanting to disturb the perfect scene. Taking my putter out of my bag was almost a disturbance and I found myself trying to do this quietly. In those moments everything seemed perfect and there was almost an inevitability about the putt rolling into the hole. The ball confidently following the script. An unexpected four.

Chapter 13

The Thirteenth

Let the nothingness into your swing.
Michael Murphy – *Golf in the Kingdom*

'Watch!' he said, rather urgently.

As I look round, a skylark stops singing and drops like a stone from the sky, stopping sharply a few inches above the ground. Although I've seen this many times before I'm still convinced that it will crash into the earth. The little scene breaks the spell I'm under and I realise how completely immersed I am in the game, to the exclusion of almost everything around me. I'm once again certain that he knows this and that his intervention was a quite deliberate attempt to awaken me from my trance.

I am immediately reminded of a dream.

In it I'm playing golf and my partner knocks his ball into deep water. To my surprise he goes to retrieve it and completely submerges himself, including his clubs, until he disappears from view.

By the time we get to the next tee I'm taking in the next hole and the view, which is spectacular. A whole panorama of grassy hillocks, water beyond and green hills beyond that. The tee is high up on a hill and exposed to the breeze. The only thing between the tee and the green, which is a little plateau, at eye level, 150 yards away, is a deep hollow of thick tussocky grass. Anything hit short is in that grass and good night, Irene! Same as anything hit left or right. At the back of the green is a little bank that might save you if you go too far. As Arnold Palmer once said, a hole 'designed by God'.

'You have to try to hit your ball from this little shelf to that little shelf over there?' he asked in a quaint way highlighting the difficulty of the shot which is already intimidating whatever level you play at.

The difference was that this time I was also seeing the bigger picture. The stunning view, wind in my hair, beautiful day to be alive, heart beating not only with fear but some excitement and a sense of what does it really matter if I **** it up?

I looked into my bag for a seven iron but it was hiding and the eight was prominent as if saying 'No, take me!'

I went with the intuition rather than the thought (I was learning!). The seven-iron thought was probably infused with a bit of fear of the 'whatever you do don't be short!' variety.

I made a fairly relaxed swing, in the circumstances, and the ball flew high and straight. From this point its fate is in the lap of the gods. It was high enough to be in their laps! Although the swing was fairly carefree, now the result started to matter.

'Go! Go!' I implored, as if this made a blind bit of difference to the outcome.

Eventually it landed, two feet onto the front of the green, hopped up and stayed near its pitch mark. I felt a warm glow of satisfaction.

He must have spotted the smug grin on my face as he said, 'I think it was your Rudyard Kipling who said beware the two imposters: triumph and disaster.'

'Spoilsport,' I said, half under my breath.

'It doesn't mean we can't enjoy our successes but just don't allow them to feed the ego. It will never be satisfied. You'll end up on a roller coaster of good and bad and to quote another of your great writers, Hamlet says "there is nothing either good or bad, but thinking makes it so."'

I could see how what he said allowed a freedom from the roller coaster. But it seemed to involve such a significant letting go of the highs and lows. Rehab for the drama junkie.

I'd already had glimpses of freedom, of a letting go and the peacefulness of a quiet walk and a golf swing without pressure.

After years and years of competitive sport could I really let that attitude go? Even the card and board games we played at home when I was a kid were fought tooth and nail. Losing was shameful, with no escape other than to make sure you win next time.

Shameful now seems such a strong word for the feeling of losing at Scrabble or Monopoly, for example. It is, of course, but that **was** the feeling. There was no other word for it!

Something drew me to the idea of being off this roller coaster, while, at the same time, being aware of how tough it would be to let go of the highs and the lows. They are both imposters but the love/hate/fascination was strong and binding. The rush of the drug in the veins was enticing and when the drug is absent the longing can demand the next rush be injected as soon as possible.

These thoughts rattled around as we took the narrow path around the hollow to the green. It was quite a steep drop into the hollow so the walk required some concentration. I'd have to come back to this quandary. Perhaps I wasn't ready to let go anyway. I could carry on bathing in my prowess at achieving such a precise shot. Or maybe I couldn't carry on – perhaps the seed had been planted.

The walk was sheltered by the hill, so, as we got to the green, the breeze struck my face. Going over to my ball I looked back over the hollow to the tee. Was that another glow of pride? The tee, the only piece of cut grass in view, looked tiny on the other side of the hollow. I felt slightly dizzy.

The putt I was left with must have been 25 feet and the thought of a birdie on this wonderful hole added some urgency into the stroke. The ball was on line but too speedy to take the slight break. It cruised past, ending up about five feet beyond the hole. Now the thoughts went from 'be great to birdie this' to 'don't three putt after that tee shot!' providing yet another example of the thought affecting the swing or putting stroke.

The result this time was what in golfing terms is called a 'yip', where the hands make an involuntary jerky movement.

The outcome is never good with the ball usually heading off way right of the hole. '****!' I thought with a mixture of anger and fear. This was not always a one-off affliction. I'd had a time playing where this affected every short putt for months. The yips had ended some stellar professional careers. And some, notably Bernhard Langer, had cured themselves to become brilliant masters of the game within a game.

Fortunately, I'd not jerked the ball too far from the hole and could tap in before thinking too long about the next one.

What was that about both triumph and disaster being imposters? Nice theory, but at this moment disaster seemed very real and was spoiling the experience of this beautiful golf hole.

I looked at Ram. There was a hint of a smile around his lips. Or was it a smirk. Unusually, I held his gaze for a little longer... or did he hold mine?

Chapter 14

The Fourteenth

There's a fine line between humility and humiliation.
Emily Ruppert, psychotherapist

The fourteenth is one of those links holes that looks a little like the face of the moon. All you can see from the tee is a sea of humps and hollows stretching out randomly in front of you. Some golfers prefer the manicured grass and well-defined fairways of a parkland course. Links golf is an acquired taste and not for everyone. There is a story of Arnold Palmer's first experience of links golf at Troon in 1962. Apparently, in the practice round he drilled a drive straight down the middle of the fairway. On landing, it hit one of the aforementioned types of humps, sending the ball spiralling sideways and scurrying into deep rough.

His frustrated comment was apparently something along the lines of 'that ain't fair' as he walked off the course. Palmer had been used to target golf in the States where the ball bounces straight and stays where it lands on the soft, well-watered fairways and greens. Like the true champion he was, he decided to adapt his game to this different environment and so successfully that he won the Open that year at Troon at his first attempt.

At least Palmer had the experience of seeing what happened to his ball. My drive across the moonscape disappeared over hump number one, reappearing briefly between humps three, four and five, like a kid on a roller coaster without the screams.

We followed the line of the drive as we walked but, as with Palmer's experience, the humps and bumps had moved it some 20 yards off line. It was nestling in some semi-rough grass just off the fairway, near enough to a yellow gorse bush to drink in its sweet smell.

It was left with a five iron to the green into a slight breeze. The thought of the breeze was enough to add just a little urgency into the down swing sending the ball hooking high and left. Did someone once say we learn by repetition?

This time my ball had gone through the semi-rough into the thicker stuff and nearly into a gorse bush, close enough for me to have to stand against the prickly bush and for the backswing to be severely restricted. Not being allowed to hit the bush in the practice swing, I practised a short choppy swing in the hope of a good contact. The actual swing was similar and the heavy head of the sand iron made a good contact, getting the ball to the front apron of the huge green.

The green, which itself sloped wickedly, lay on the other side of the huge hill that was in front of me. I couldn't even see the top of the pin from where I stood next to my ball. I glanced at my friend and thought I detected the faintest hint of a smile around his lips.

Putting seemed the best option, as taking a wedge would run the risk of not getting enough height on the shot and catching the bank. A putt would still involve sound judgement.

However, maybe because of the difficulty of the shot I tried to make this judgement with my head rather than my body. During the backswing I thought 'this is a big hit' closely followed by 'better not overdo it'. With the second thought I decelerated through the ball, which scampered up the steep slope but soon ran out of steam. It 'struck camp' for a second, three feet from the summit and descended in disgrace to report home inches from where it had been dispatched.

His laughter filled my ears.

'You are back where you started,' he managed to say between giggles.

I was surprised at my reaction to his mirth. Usually I feel the prickly competitive edge that goes with the laugh. Golfers either laugh in triumph, sometimes including some black humour as in shouting 'Dead sheep!' (meaning still ewe/you to play your shot again) or more often respecting the moment with silence or saying 'bad luck'; as though witnessing a tragic occurrence. Perhaps we do not dare join in with the self-humiliation that already exists in the heart of the perpetrator and we know that next time it could be us.

His laugh was one born of humility rather than humiliation. I knew from hearing him that he could laugh at himself whilst still honouring something precious inside. I also felt he was not laughing at me and was inviting me to learn another way.

I had been brought up by teachers many of whom thought that to shame the pupil was the best way to drive him to better results.

I now had this as a part of me and often brought it to the golf course. I realised that I had a choice with this type of 'failure' to berate myself for my stupidity or learn a lesson whilst dealing with myself in a compassionate way. After all, I had done my best at the time.

I understood also that this affected my second attempt. The berated pupil may try too hard from fear or may rebel. The fear, however, does often generate the alertness and motivation to get the job done. No one wants to be exposed to shame in front of his peers.

The pupil treated with compassion, however, will learn responsively, trusting his capacities. I had believed this as an idea, but this was a lesson in experience.

This time I practised the shot whilst looking at where the ball was going (a Jack Nicklaus tip for long putts) getting the feel for the distance in my hands and body. The ball reached the summit this time, paused, and trickled over the top, out of sight, running gently down to the flag.

* * *

As we walked around the slope to the green, the sea beyond the next hole came into view. The long wispy grasses were dancing in the now vigorous breeze. In that moment I saw in them a lightness and ease of movement that I felt inside me. It was like a glimpse of an inner world of self-acceptance; of just being; a light open-heartedness and free spirit. His compassion had touched me lightly but deeply.

The fast downhill six-foot putt with the nine-inch break was so easy in this state of bliss that I only realised I had been involved in it when the dull rattle of the ball in the cup woke me gently.

This last lesson led me to think about how I had been taught through most of my life. We tend to think that information passed on is learning. This teacher/friend knew himself and who he was in the world, and he was teaching me things through his being. This was not just having knowledge this was being knowledge.

Chapter 15

The Fifteenth

It just shows you how sometimes when you let your guard down or you let your expectations soften, you can free yourself up.

Harrison Frazar, (who had considered quitting the tour, battled back from hip surgery and missed five successive cuts before regaining his form)

The fifteenth is short par four (264 yards) with the beach lying all along the left-hand side and just beyond the green. The beach, which is out of bounds, is only four yards from the green. Short and to the right of the green are a little line of bunkers protecting the putting surface.

There was an intense smell of seaweed and the gentle crackle of sea on pebbles. In the distance an oil tanker was just visible in the sea mist.

The wind was helping so I decided on the driver.

I was starting to be aware of holes running out and my limited time with Ram. Who'd have thought this would be true after all the irritation at the beginning of the round?

I was keen to perfect the lessons that he had introduced me to and made a special effort on this difficult drive. This was a great opportunity as the result on this hole is classic risk and reward. So, what had I learnt? Trust the swing. Don't care what happens, process not outcome.

I set up for a slight fade and reminded myself to trust the body and decades of golf swings. This worked perfectly until I got to the top of the swing where doubt sneaked in and tightened a whole group of muscles. The effect was more of a steer than a swing. The ball came out of the heel of the club and headed for the beach quicker than a German tourist booking his sun lounger. It collided with a rock, narrowly missing a feeding oystercatcher, flying miles in the air and out of sight. Out of bounds. Playing three off the tee.

With a mixture of annoyance and disappointment I reloaded. What was different today was that I could let the annoyance be there but not overwhelm me. So often the feelings would be still bubbling during the next shot. In fact, this time I remembered the feeling of doubt and the tight steery swing with acceptance. This allowed me to know what was **not** relaxed or peaceful about the last swing and to have a memory of the absence of tightness and the subtle need to control.

I set up again in the same way; this time the swing was free and relaxed. Maybe this was a mixture of the memory of a carefree swing and that it's always easier the second time around. The ball came out of the middle of the club face and hugged the shoreline for 180 yards or so before climbing and moving right in the air, mimicking the shape of the hole. It took a couple of good bounces and came up just short of the green.

The fear of running out of time compelled me to ask Ram a question.

'I think I understand what you've been trying to teach me today but it's not easy to put into practice? I thought once I'd got it that would be it. That those thoughts wouldn't bother me again.'

'It is true that once we know this wisdom, it cannot be unknown,' he began.

'But there is a momentum in the old patterns. You can turn the wheel on an oil tanker but it can take some time for it to change direction. In some ways the patterns never leave us but just have less influence. The strong lines become faint like on tracing paper,' he said.

'What about the needs of the ego to win or play well?' I asked.

'My teacher's teacher once said that with this practice ego becomes like the moon on a bright summer's day: present but incidental.'

'So, what do we do about the old patterns and about ego?'

'There is nothing to do. Simply accept whatever's there and they will dissolve in your awareness. Like a sugar lump in liquid.'

'Thank you,' I said, not entirely sure what I was thanking him for. But beyond the words there was a softening in my body and mind and a feeling of peacefulness. It was like his words were pointing beyond the words at this sense of peace each time he spoke, inviting my attention away from the foreground to the background. Resting there for a while, I did not want to interrupt the experience with more words.

A large herring gull floated past, needing only one gentle flap of its wings to send it way out to sea.

I got to my ball. Even that seemed to be quietly waiting my arrival.

I was left with a shot of about 60 yards, but flat all the way and with no hazards in between. I decided to go with a seven-wood pitch. It's a shot that can work well if you remember to play it like a putt and that the ball jumps off the face of the club somewhat. I made a good enough putting stroke and the ball made a little clack-type noise off the club. It jumped about an inch off the ground for a couple of feet then rolled and rolled toward the hole. Having looked like it might stop near the hole, my ball carried on and on finally coming to a halt about eight feet past the pin. The putt back was true and on line just deviating slightly as it approached the hole catching the left lip. From there it spun round the whole cup and entered from the place it first started.

Bogey five but birdie with second ball. Was that any consolation? Perhaps, but only slight. And then again, did it matter?

Chapter 16

The Sixteenth

I left my mind blank for my body to act.
Emilio Butragueño (Real Madrid legend who scored 171 goals in a 12-year spell at the Bernabéu and became known as 'El Buitre' – the vulture – when asked the key to his success)

The sixteenth hole is a par four with a sharp dog leg left. As you stand on the tee there is a wonderful view of the long beach. The first part of the hole runs parallel to the sea and then turns sharply left inland.

'Where are you supposed to hit your ball?' asked Ram.

There are many occasions on a links golf course where you can stand over a shot with little or no idea where you're going. You can be faced with a sea of humps and bumps and no sign of the cut grass that you're hoping to find.

'Over the marker post,' I said.

'Oh, the little stripy post on that hill?'

'That's the one.'

With a sharp dog leg, you need to be careful to take the right club. A perfect straight hit with a driver can take you right over the fairway into deep undergrowth. Also, the wind will be a big factor. Wind in your face and even a driver might not take you over the marker post; again a good shot leaving you in deep rough. Today with the breeze off the sea, a well hit 3 wood should fly the ball over the hill with the marker post on it and, with luck, the wind should help it left along the dog leg. Well, that's the idea.

I was learning from Ram not to overthink this, so having had the thought about the shot needed, I parked this and all thoughts about the outcome, leaving only the process and a carefree swing.

A few thoughts were left rumbling around – Was this the right club? Is the breeze getting up? Keep your head down! Don't go on the beach! Don't overcompensate and go left! – all reminding me of a joke video I'd seen once called 'The 57 things to remember during the golf swing'.

The memory brought a lightness to such a serious matter which made the carefree nature of it easier. Perhaps that's why Lee Trevino was cracking jokes all the way round even in the major competitions.

The swing was easy, the strike was good and the ball sailed over the marker, rose a bit and veered left on the breeze, accentuating the spin on it. We didn't see the ball land but it looked about right.

As we walked over the hillock where the rough becomes fairway and my ball came within view, I realised that I was not overly concerned about its fate. Before the experience of this round I would have been agitating about my lie and my approach shot. Now I felt a deep sense of contentment and the simple joy of the salty breeze and the reassuring crash of the waves on the pebble beach. I was no longer reliant on good shots or outcomes but was in touch with the real reason that I played this wonderful game.

This was my coming home. Coming home to Nature to the source of all things. To judge how hard to hit a wedge shot of 86 yards was not a matter of technique but a matter of immersion in the natural world, of feeling the distance, of being the space between you and the pin. To stand and viscerally compute the wind strength to 'know' how hard to hit the little sphere.

There was some loss to my precious ego and of the reward to that fragile part of me that wanted to know that 'I' had hit a good shot. Now this felt more like the shots equated with my capacity to get in the flow and rhythm of my environment. Less of: me hit ball, ball fly to target, and more of: me/club/ball/target.

* * *

Francis Ouimet, the 20-year-old surprise winner of the 1913 US Open, came back to the golf course after hearing an opera singer the night before and remarking that the song seemed to come through her rather than from her. He went on to beat Harry Vardon and Ted Ray, the undisputed champions of the day with some inspired golf but was renowned for his modesty, perhaps knowing that great play was the harmony between man and a higher source.

The second shot is through the windy gap that the hole is named after. In some ways the hills on either side of the fairway gave a way of easily lining up the next shot. Being still in easy mode, the swing with a seven iron flowed nicely and the ball sailed off towards the green. Whether it was the wind behind or, as often happens, when you swing easily the ball went further than normal bouncing on the green but straight through the back.

With the pin placed right at the back of the green, the shot back was tricky. I had to get it to fly up quickly and then to land softly on the edge of the green. This called for the lob wedge: a club with usually 60 or even 64 degrees of loft which makes it look more like a flat frying pan than a golf club. The trick is to make a very full swing and let the loft on the club do the rest, hitting down rather than trying to scoop the ball up. It involved a high degree of trust.

The thought about trust reminded me of a little video clip of Phil Mickelson playing a lob wedge. This was no ordinary shot as he'd placed his caddie about five feet in front of him. Now there's trust! Mickelson takes a full swing and the ball pops up almost vertically, over the caddie's head and lands softly behind him.

The image of this trick shot from the master of the lob wedge was helpful, giving me the confidence to make a full, easy swing and hit down slightly.

The ball popped up obediently and landed softly on the fringe, trickling down to the hole, stopping barely six inches short. Tap in par.

High risk – high reward. Where does that phrase sit in the realm of not caring what happens?

Chapter 17

The Seventeenth

The ego is thus in permanent conflict, at once longing for its own oblivion in oneness and at the same time habitually fighting for its very existence.

Jean Klein, non-dual teacher, *I Am*

The seventeenth is another hole where the driver is not the wisest choice for the average golfer – unless you can carry the ball 270 yards over the burn that runs across the hole. The five wood seemed the right choice. Hit well, even with a following wind, the ball should end up short of the hazard.

I like my five wood. It sits nicely on the ground and invites a smooth strike. I sometimes think I'm more accurate with it than a wedge. Add to this the quiet sense of well-being that had become more of an ongoing experience and the swing replicated the mood. The ball flew off high and straight, only going right on landing, taking two or three little hops into the light rough.

We set off down the path to the fairway and Ram began another chapter in the lecture tour.

'Your game is a great teacher. You imagine there is someone called "you" playing and succeeding and failing. But there is really no such thing as an individual.'

Responding to my frown he carried on.

'For example, how can you call something a tree and talk about it in isolation? A tree cannot be a tree without air, earth, light, water, birds and other elements. In the same way, thinking of yourself as a separate person is an illusion. And our ego is part of that illusion: it imagines itself to be in control and master of its environment – not the servant. Usually manipulating each situation for its own ends. Even now, your ego is probably thinking how it can use this to become a better golfer.'

'What do you mean?'

If I'd asked this question at the beginning of the round it would've had much more of an edge to it. Perhaps a bit of aggression. This time it came from a real sense of wanting to understand more.

'Even today what you call "you" has hit some shots that went very well so that ego, the "controller", can use these to imagine it now has the answer. Paradoxically, the answer is the dissolution of ego, and the illusion of the separate self. It's as if the individual wave falls back into the ocean and realises that it was never separate, never not the ocean,' Ram explained.

Once again, I remembered my years of playing football. The most enjoyable memories were those of being part of a team. Each of us an important cog in the machine. Playing our best when in tune with each other like a machine that had been well-oiled. Memories of the energy in the dressing room before the game. The beer and the post-match analysis. The lasting friendships born of joint endeavour. As they say, there's no 'I' in team.

'Your beautiful game provides you with so many reminders that you are part of everything,' he went on.

'You imagine you control the flight of the ball and work out the distance with your brain, but the controller is an imposter. Your good shots, as you call them, are the natural outcome of you being one with your environment. Of course, you need a technique to hit the ball. I could not do this. But once able to cause the ball to fly straight and high, your only practice is to let go and be one with the natural world around you. Your body will then remember a different type of knowing that existed before the controller, your ego, assumed its throne. Take today, for example.' His words were flowing now.

'So, what about today?' I asked.

'We could say that two individuals randomly meet up and

talk to each other about what they love. You introduce me to your passion for this game and I point you to another way of seeing your sport and life in general. But this is not how things really are. It is more like oneness bringing two aspects of itself together at the same time. Synchronicity!'

'I think I get that. But how would it apply to our example today?'

'Well, for one thing, you could not have understood what has been said unless it was already known and you were open to being reminded.'

'Whoa!' I said, as if trying to get a horse to slow down.

'And you and your game have reminded me of the power of the mind and the ultimate power of Nature.' he said.

'But Ram, you seem to already know this stuff anyway.'

'That's how it seems to a mind used to seeing a world full of separate objects.' he explained. He paused and looked over at me.

'It appears to the mind that this individual me passes something on to you, another separate individual. Two separate trees in the same forest. But we know now that trees communicate via their root systems. However, the mind cannot see the tree in its full glory, its perfect interconnectedness. In the same way that true wisdom comes from beyond the individual and, like today, infuses us both with its fragrance.'

I was struggling to grasp what he was saying but at the same time felt a deeper knowing beyond any words. Again, as if reading my mind, he went on.

'Interconnectedness is beyond the realm of the mind. This can only be experienced and may only occasionally be glimpsed when the mind is still and the being remembers its own true source. Maybe, this is why you play this wonderful game?'

There didn't seem to be any words that quite worked for this moment, but I was rescued by our arrival at my ball, which sat invitingly in the soft grass of the first cut of rough a few feet from the fairway.

I was faced with a shot of just over 210 yards, downwind, the green set through a little alley of pot bunkers. The alley angled slightly to the right as it approached the green. Because I was on the right side of the fairway the ball would need to move from left to right in the air if it was going to find its way to the green. With mind and ego now demoted from master to servant, I simply looked softly at the whole image: at the fairway, the bunkers and the green, just taking it all in without thought or intention. Fading the ball (moving it left to right) was not my natural shot, although perhaps a little easier with the 21-degree rescue club I'd chosen for the task in hand.

Absorbing the totality of the experience, I allowed the shape of my body in the stance to be in tune with the lie of the land and the space around it.

The swing was easy and my little white dimpled friend set off low towards the left-hand bunkers, climbed a bit and moved calmly in the air to the right. It bounced softly on the apron of the green and skipped up on to the dance floor – as the green is affectionately known in some circles.

We walked in a peaceful silence for half the journey to the green and then a question came.

'I think I get some sense of all this but if the mind can't grasp what you're describing, what do I do?'

'Just notice the ego,' said Ram. 'Notice how many thoughts are centred around the self. As you observe these thoughts, enquire into whether they are really you. For example, some people think they are better than others and some think they are worth less than others. Neither of these thoughts are true.

'The same with you. You will see your thoughts are not who you are. As you see this, your true self is revealed. There is no doing just noticing. All effort then becomes irrelevant as there are no steps to take to who you are.' He paused. 'You told me that the ball flies further when there is no effort, no attempt to use force, so, in life, no effort is needed to be who we truly are,' he said. 'When the tensions and strivings are observed they dissolve and a natural stillness and relaxation are revealed.'

Wow! this seemed a lot to take in, but I thought about how wonderfully easy that last shot felt; how the mind and ego might have intervened to make things difficult. Also, how easy it was to simply allow this sort of knowing without trying to grasp, dissect or analyse.

When this thought subsided, there was just walking: the ease of each step and each breath simply following another. I felt the warmth of the sun on my neck.

The green is big and sloping. No more dew left on the surface so now really slick. Fortunately, my putt from 30 feet or so was uphill and I could make a nice smooth stroke rolling the ball to about a foot. Par four.

Chapter 18

The Eighteenth

We shall not cease from exploration
And the end of all our exploring
Will be to arrive where we started
And know the place for the first time.
T.S. Eliot, 'Little Gidding', *Four Quartets*

The final hole, the eighteenth, is a testing par four dog leg to the right with the green sitting just in front of the clubhouse and the quiet chatter of post-round analysis.

The ideal shape for this final drive is a fade, opening up the green for the next shot. The usual anxious anticipation was only there as a faint line on tracing paper. The conversations and experiences we'd been having led me without any intention to a mind empty of thought. Not only was the mind empty but it was as though there was no one playing. Making this final tee shot there was swinging but no one engaged in that activity. The swing took place without 'me'. The swing was also in complete union with the terrain, and the ball followed the shape of the fairway as it turned sharply to the right after 200 yards, climbed and landed softly in the centre of the fairway around 260 yards from the tee. Normally this sort of result would have left me in some way proud of what I had achieved. 'I' had made a good shot, etc. This time there was no sense of me, no glow of achievement. This time only a oneness. A swinging, flying, body, club, ball, landing, air, sky, grass experience. Joyous, but not the sort of pleasure where the ego feels inflated.

After all the years of golf, here was in these moments a different sort of knowing. My mind could not really grasp the notion of no one playing; but the deep questioning of who was playing allowed an opening to this knowledge, to a wisdom beyond mind and intellect.

'Mushin,' Ram said, out of the blue.

'Pardon?' I said, not sure if this was speech or a muffled sneeze.

'Mushin means "no mind". In the practice of Zen and archery. Mushin, which is not technique, solves the paradox of the release. Mushin allows one to transcend technique and intuit the naturally correct way of letting the string release itself from the hand. In this way, the release is neither purposeful nor purposeless.'

'Why didn't you tell me all this at the beginning of the round?'

'Because once you have the technique there is no progress to be made. But we need to think there is in order to realise that there never was any progress to make.'

Although to one part of me frustrating, I knew there was something profound about what he had said. It spoke to me at some level beyond thought. In fact, my mind could not make sense of it in the ordinary way that we try and understand, although by this stage I was no longer fighting with the things I couldn't immediately understand.

* * *

My drive had ended up right in the middle of the fairway. I only had about 130 yards to the pin. Normally a nine iron. Uphill an eight.

With the clubhouse just behind the green, there was often the thought that a shot hit thin might fly hard and low, straight over the green and bounce amongst the lager shandies and ginger beers. I had the thought but just watched it with some amusement.

The lightness of the moment was in the swing as well and the ball flew high towards the green landing on the front, a good way short of the hole.

As we walked up to green, I wondered what it was like at the end of the Open Championship to walk up the last green surrounded by thousands of people.

A friend of mine had done this many years ago. As English Boy's Amateur Champion he had been invited to play in the Open and had holed his second shot into the last green accompanied by the roar of the crowd. He didn't say whether anyone had shouted 'Get in the hole!' on his backswing as is the custom in America. Sadly, this was his eightieth shot and his only Open.

I had left myself a putt which was a long way up the green to the pin. I spent some time over it hoping to get a feel for the distance. Like many uphill putts it appeared at the halfway point to be going too fast, but the slope kicked in and put its brakes on. It arrived at the pin only a little steamy and hit it full on but with enough momentum to bounce it back against the rim of the hole. It popped up, staying on the front lip.

I looked up, having been engrossed in this final scene, to see whether Ram had been watching. But he was nowhere to be seen. He'd gone. For a moment I even wondered for a second whether I had imagined him and had just been having a three-hour conversation inside my head.

I walked back to my bag a little deflated only to find a tiny old battered book balanced against my clubs. On the front there was an old Yin/Yang symbol, below the title 'Zen Poems'. Inside there was a message.

'For Martin,
Namaste, Ram.'

I read the first poem:

Intention is
In Tension.

Chapter 19

The Nineteenth

But now the physical body moves within the expanded body and the movements appear in a new way. It is important not to let the conditioned sensations take over again, but to knowingly sustain the feeling of emptiness.
Jean Klein, *I Am*

Having changed my shoes and gone to the bar, I took my pint of bitter outside and sat next to the old clubhouse and looked out to sea. My seat had a little plaque with the faded name of a member who had died over 40 years ago. Perhaps this was his favourite spot.

A pair of gannets was fishing out to sea. Folding their wings and plunging steeply into water from 30 feet or so.

I'd sat there many times, usually chatting with my golfing partners, immersed in post-mortems and of what might have been.

This time I was more aware of the silence. Not as in the absence of sound but a silent background to everything, including in some way me. Not surprisingly, this could not be put into words and in these moments I did not try. Everything just was as it was and nothing needed to be added. It was extraordinary and completely ordinary. It had always been there, I just had not seen it. It reminded me of the optical illusion drawing which can either be seen as a vase or two faces looking at each other. We're shown the drawing and can only see the vase and not the faces. No amount of effort helps us see the faces but once seen, perhaps out of the corner of the eye, we cannot not see them.

Life was simply happening and, shockingly I was not the centre of it. I was one tiny pebble on the beach. But paradoxically, in the moments when 'me' fell away, there was belonging, humility and a dissolving of a sense of other, of separateness.

There was only simple solitude but not loneliness.

The words 'just this' arose gently in my mind.

I picked up Ram's book of poems. It fell open at another poem.

Nothing to do
Nowhere to go
No one to be.

Epilogue

Two weeks after the round with Ram, I had a phone call from my brother.

Tony said, 'I played in a competition for the first time in weeks yesterday. As you know I've had a bad back. It was still a bit sore yesterday.'

'How did you get on?' I asked.

'Played my best golf for years! Finished with a net 66. Because of my back I played with no expectation.'

'That sounds great. That's just what my guy, Ram, was talking about.'

'Who the **** is Ram?'

'The guy who walked round with me when you were ill.'

'Oh yeah! Well that's a bit spooky.'

'Just a bit,' I said.

'The next time I play I'm going to try to do the same again.'

'Good luck with that!' I said without thinking about it. The words spilled out like a recording of Ram's voice, with the slightest hint of his accent and of the delightful movement of his head from side to side, which fortunately my brother could not see.

'What do you mean?'

'Just that you can't try not to try. Then we just create a new expectation!'

'Bloody hell!'

'I know, infuriating isn't it. I found a poem in the little book he gave me. It sort of helped.'

The efficacy of trying is revealed to be like
Catching the wind in a sieve.
Wu Hsin

The realisations from this day would stay with me, not just on the golf course but in every aspect of life. Without making deliberate changes I was more accepting of what life brought – much less controlling of what could not be controlled and therefore at peace with the way things were.

On the golf course and elsewhere the outcome was now less important. Winning didn't come with the same highs and losing was less painful.

I still got angry sometimes at a poor shot or the mind getting in the way, but these were now like a sneeze, over and done with in seconds as opposed to the former two- or three-hole grumpiness.

I could more easily spot the mind's attempts to interrupt what is natural, both during the golf swing and in life. I could also observe the workings of my ego both on and off the course and came to really understand the notion of no one playing. I started to feel the difference between understanding this as a concept and knowing it. Started living it! How the absence of ego allowed a freedom and allowed defensiveness and aggression to dissolve.

I could still enjoy competition but now it was less attached to self-esteem.

I came to know a fundamental stillness present in everything. Not a literal stillness, but what we might experience watching the most effortless movements in sport and in Nature – as when the eagle soars across the sky.

About the Author

Martin Wells has worked as a psychotherapist in the NHS in the West of England for over 30 years. He has also been teaching mindfulness to patients and staff for most of that time. Twelve years ago his own profound experience of 'letting go' radically changed the way he lives and works. Since then a non-dual perspective has informed his psychotherapy and mindfulness teaching and practice, his relationships and his overall approach to life.

As a young man, Martin played golf for Hertfordshire and, although now 70, is still a single figure handicap golfer. He also played senior amateur and semi-professional football for nearly 20 years.

Martin lives in Bristol with his wife, Sue. Their two daughters and three grandchildren live nearby.

Books by the author

Sitting in the Stillness
Mantra books, John Hunt Publishing, 2020
ISBN 978-1-78904-266-5

What if there is, fundamentally, nothing to change or fix in ourselves?

Sitting in the Stillness is a collection of stories from the therapy room. Each one invites the reader to go beyond these personal accounts to the universal, beyond the agitations of the mind to an infinite stillness of being. The stories include examples from group therapy, mindfulness groups, family and couples' therapy and demonstrate our fundamental interconnectedness.

Author's note

Each of the 18 holes in the book corresponds to an actual hole from an unnamed course in England, Scotland or Ireland. For example, the first hole is the actual first hole on one of these courses. There is one exception: the 3rd hole is actually the 4th on a course in Cornwall – (a clue here because I messed it up!).

The first reader that can name all 18 will be treated by the author to a round of golf and a pint afterwards.

References

Eliot, T.S. (1943) *The Four Quartets,* Faber and Faber, London

Freud, S. (2012) *A General Introduction to Psychoanalysis,* Wordsworth editions; Classic World literature edition

Hesse, Herman. (1981) *Siddartha,* Bantham books, New York, USA, (first published 1922)

Klein, Jean. (2016) *I Am,* Non-Duality Press, UK

Melvyn, R. (2001) *The Lost Writings of Wu Hsin,* Summa Iru Publishing, Boulder, Colorado, USA

Murphy, M. (1992) *Golf in the Kingdom,* Penguin Compass, New York, USA

Niebauer, Chris. (2019) *No Self no Problem: How Neuropsychology is Catching up to Buddhism,* Hierophant Publishing, USA

Ruppert, Emily. (2017) *Rebels and Sweethearts,* Transactional Analysis Journal Vol. 47 Number 3

Vardon, Harry. (1905) *The Complete Golfer,* Sand Sedge Publishers, Wrexham, UK

Whitman, Walt. (1855) *Leaves of Grass,* Dover Thrift editions, USA

Appendix: Web based resources

https://mantel.pro – Dr Jean-Marc Mantel's website with many articles, talks and meditations on non-duality.

https://www.non-dualmindfulness.com – the authors own website with information about retreats, meetings and links to articles and interviews.

https://shivas.org – a website dedicated to keeping alive the philosophy that inspired Michael Murphy's classic book: *Golf in the Kingdom*.

The Less Dust the More Trust
Participating in The Shamatha Project, Meditation and Science
Adeline van Waning, MD PhD
The inside-story of a woman participating in frontline meditation research, exploring the interfaces of mind-practice, science and psychology.
Paperback: 978-1-78099-948-7 ebook: 978-1-78279-657-2

I Know How To Live, I Know How To Die
The Teachings of Dadi Janki: A warm, radical, and life-affirming view of who we are, where we come from, and what time is calling us to do
Neville Hodgkinson
Life and death are explored in the context of frontier science and deep soul awareness.
Paperback: 978-1-78535-013-9 ebook: 978-1-78535-014-6

Living Jainism
An Ethical Science
Aidan Rankin, Kanti V. Mardia
A radical new perspective on science rooted in intuitive awareness and deductive reasoning.
Paperback: 978-1-78099-912-8 ebook: 978-1-78099-911-1

Ordinary Women, Extraordinary Wisdom
The Feminine Face of Awakening
Rita Marie Robinson
A collection of intimate conversations with female spiritual teachers who live like ordinary women, but are engaged with their true natures.
Paperback: 978-1-84694-068-2 ebook: 978-1-78099-908-1

The Way of Nothing
Nothing in the Way
Paramananda Ishaya
A fresh and light-hearted exploration of the amazing reality of
nothingness.
Paperback: 978-1-78279-307-6 ebook: 978-1-78099-840-4

Readers of ebooks can buy or view any of these bestsellers by
clicking on the live link in the title. Most titles are published in
paperback and as an ebook. Paperbacks are available in traditional
bookshops. Both print and ebook formats are available online.

Find more titles and sign up to our readers' newsletter at
http://www.johnhuntpublishing.com/mind-body-spirit.
Follow us on Facebook at https://www.facebook.com/OBooks
and Twitter at https://twitter.com/obooks.